ALTERNATIVES FOR THE PROBLEM DRINKER

A.A. is not the only way

Ariel Winters

DRAKE PUBLISHERS INC.
NEW YORK · LONDON

Dedicated to my daughter,

Laurie Anne Williams Brown

Published in 1978 by
Drake Publishers, Inc.
801 Second Avenue
New York, N.Y. 10017

Library of Congress Cataloging in Publication Data

Winters, Ariel.
    Alternatives for the problem drinker.

    Bibliography: p.
    Includes index.
    1. Alcoholism. I. Title.
RC565.W57   616.8'61   77-87466
ISBN 0-8473-1701-3

Design: Harold Franklin

Printed in the United States of America

CONTENTS

ACKNOWLEDGMENTS

The author acknowledges with gratitude the following persons for their inspiration, encouragement, suggestions, or other help in the preparation of this book:

John Cashman

Diana Speedwell

Ted Gottfried

Bob Decker

Dr. M. A. Hartman

Dr. William Miller

Dr. Roger Vogler

Drs. Linda and Mark Sobell

The Drinkwatchers Advisory Board

And the over 30,000 persons all over the world who wrote Drinkwatchers seeking an alternative.

Preface

by **William R. Miller, Ph.D.**
(Author of "How to Control Your Drinking")

Few health problems today receive as much public attention as is currently devoted to alcoholism and problem drinking. Each daily newspaper tells us of new discoveries about "the cause" of problem drinking, of new legislation about alcohol, of alcohol-related crimes and social problems, and of new "miracle cures" for alcoholism. At least a dozen professional journals are devoted to research on alcohol and addictive behaviors, and hundreds of books and articles about alcohol are published each year. The federal government spends millions annually to support research and treatment of problem drinkers.

And rightfully so! Recent research indicates that about 9% of our adult population have several significant life problems directly related to the use of alcohol, and so may be reasonably termed "problem drinkers." If, as other research has indicated, each problem drinker closely affects the lives of three other people on the average, then perhaps a third of our population are directly touched.

The fact is that we still know relatively little about alcohol and alcoholism. Little is understood of how alcohol produces addiction or even intoxication. Recent research suggests that many phenomena we once attributed directly to the chemical action of alcohol—aggression, sexual behavior, released inhibitions, loss of control—may be due instead to a much more complicated combination of psychological, physiological, and social factors surrounding drinking. Many treatment approaches are offered to problem drinkers, but very few of these are based upon research demonstrating their effectiveness. We are unable, on present knowledge, to predict whether or how an individual will respond to the various treatment methods available.

5

This is changing. During the past ten years research has *begun* to provide some answers to these and other questions. It is now clear, for example, that all treatment methods are not equally effective (or ineffective). The physical effects of overdrinking are becoming better understood. Some of the important causes of problem drinking—and it seems there are many—are gradually being defined, and as a result new treatment approaches are being developed.

With some of these new approaches has come a not-so-new realization: that total abstinence is not the *only* answer for *all* problem drinkers. A wide range of therapeutic techniques have been developed to help people control their use of alcohol without stopping completely. This idea—that some problem drinkers can successfully moderate their drinking—proved surprisingly controversial. The substance of this controversy is well detailed by Ariel Winters in subsequent chapters. In general, controlled drinking was denounced as a "cruel hoax," with the assertion that moderation could at best be only temporary for the alcoholic, leading ultimately to relapse and further deterioration.

These concerns are well-taken. Psychologists and physicians are all too familiar with the phenomenon of the "new cure" that appears promising at first but ultimately proves dismally ineffective. The responsible scientist avoids prematurely accepting new solutions as surely as he or she avoids dogmatism that prevents new solutions from being considered.

It is also clear that there are individuals, call them alcoholics if you will, for whom complete and lifelong abstinence is the only realistic approach. Some people have medical conditions, for example liver disease, that render further drinking dangerous if not life-threatening. Others have been physiologically addicted to alcohol and face a high risk of reestablishing this addiction if they drink. Still others prove unable or unwilling, even with competent professional assistance, to maintain moderation. For such persons abstinence is the safest and easiest solution.

Still another concern voiced by professionals is that alcoholics who are now successfully abstaining will hear about controlled drinking and will decide to try it, with dire results. I share this concern. Although our knowledge about the effectiveness of controlled drinking therapies is increasing, I do not advise successful abstainers to abandon this pattern in favor of the more uncertain pursuit of moderation. Those who are doing well by abstaining are best advised to continue doing so.

There are, on the other hand, reasons for continuing to explore controlled drinking as an alternative to (but not replacement for) abstinence. There are many individuals who are unwilling to label themselves as "alcoholic" or to consider total abstinence, but who nevertheless are experiencing serious life problems related to drinking. If offered only the more traditional approaches, such persons tend to deny the severity of their problems and to avoid doing something about them. This may result in further deterioration until finally the individual "hits bottom." There is no reason to believe that such deterioration is necessary before treatment can be successful. To the contrary, our present evidence suggests that earlier treatment is more likely to succeed. It has been my experience that many individuals recognize and admit to life problems related to alcohol if they are not forced to therefore label themselves as "alcoholic," and that many are eager to do something about their drinking if moderation is a possible goal. Effective controlled drinking approaches thus may prevent the development of more severe alcohol problems.

Another reason for exploring controlled drinking therapies is the fact that abstinence-oriented approaches provide a lasting solution for only a minority of those who try them. Moderation approaches provide an alternative for those for whom abstinence methods have repeatedly failed. At this stage in our knowledge we cannot afford to discard alternatives that may be effective.

Finally there is the present body of research suggesting the effectiveness of controlled drinking approaches. In at least a dozen clinics where treatment methods with a goal of controlled drinking have been offered, substantial percentages of treated individuals— often 60% to70%— have been found to successfully learn and maintain moderate and nonproblematic drinking. Certainly more research is needed, with more long-range follow-up studies to determine which approaches are most effective for which individuals. Though far from complete and conclusive, present research certainly points to controlled drinking as a possible and promising goal for some problem drinkers.

This seems a good time for a book about "Alternatives for the Problem Drinker." There are indeed alternatives—a confusing array of them—for the person seeking either abstinence or controlled drinking. I suspect that most people who "choose" a treatment program do so on the basis of having heard about one at the right time or being referred without considering other possibilities. The idea of "shopping around" tends not to be associated with psychology and medicine. There is, however, a growing consumer awareness in these areas: that there are alternatives, that no one approach holds the answer for everyone, that approaches do differ in effectiveness, that the consumer is entitled to information about the effectiveness and cost-effectiveness of whatever she or he is offered. I am happy to see this. Perhaps it will be the public after all who require of those of us who fancy ourselves mental health professionals to ask: "How effective is this method that I am using?" and "What alternatives might be more effective or less expensive?"

William R. Miller, Ph.D.
Department of Psychology
University of New Mexico

chapter 1

Problem Drinking
as a Number One Health Problem

Alcohol is the number one drug of choice in this country. And it is legal. This ancient mood-changing substance, ethyl alcohol, has the power to induce pleasant feelings of euphoria, sedation, relaxation, and intoxication. It also reduces inhibitions. It has been used as a tranquilizer and, until modern times, served as an anesthetic. But like anything else, it can be abused, causing problems, illness, even death.

The National Institute on Alcohol Abuse and Alcoholism (NIAAA) considers a heavy drinker anyone who drinks more than one ounce of alcohol daily (about two beers). Not all heavy drinkers, they say, become alcoholics if they don't stop drinking. Light drinkers have been defined (by NIAAA) as having less than a quarter ounce of alcohol daily; moderate drinkers, up to one ounce.

Americans spend about $20 billion annually on alcoholic spirits. Modern society seems to produce in its citizens a real need for chemical comforters. (About $5 billion goes to the Federal Government in alcohol taxes.) The Department of Health, Education and Welfare says there are 9 million alcoholics in this country, or roughly one out of every ten people who drink. Congress has appropriated over one billion dollars for NIAAA since its inception, in 1971. Washingon, D.C., not surprisingly, has the highest alcoholism rate in the country. A study by American Business Men's Research Foundation of Lansing, Michigan showed that one of every five adults in the District of Columbia is an alcoholic! This may be because people who live there and work in government are under very intense pressure. Another high rate is reported among American Indians. It is twice that of the national average. (The Indians do not like to consider themselves alcoholics; victims of a white man's disease.)

9

How does drinking relate to social class? Morris Chafetz, former head of NIAAA, says: "Our statistics show that as you go up the socioeconomic ladder, there is more of a tendency to be a drinker than an abstainer. When it comes to heavy drinking, there is more in the upper classes. If you are on an assembly line and you can't do your job, the boss is going to notice in a hurry. If you're an editor of a magazine, a lot of people are just going to look the other way."

One study found that persons most likely to be *drinkers* were men and women around middle age; professional people, technical workers, salesmen, officials, managers, college graduates, and single men who reside around or in the big cities, especially those on the Pacific coast and the upper eastern seaboard. Those most likely to be *heavy drinkers* were found to be middle age persons, service workers, men who went to high school but not to college, residents of large cities, Catholics, Protestants, and those with no religious affiliation. Also single, divorced, or separated men and women.

The Department of Health, Education and Welfare recently stated that alcoholism and alcohol-related problems costs the U.S. economy more than $25 billion a year. This special report also noted that excessive alcohol consumption, when combined with smoking, may contribute to the development of certain cancers, especially those of the mouth, larynx, and esophagus.

After heart disease and cancer, alcoholism is the country's biggest health problem. There are about thirteen thousand deaths every year of cirrhosis of the liver indirectly related to alcoholism. Experts say an alcoholic's life span is shortened by from ten to twelve years. Recent evidence suggests that certain kinds of heart disease may be related to alcoholism and that alcohol, taken excessively over a period of years, can cause brain damage.

These are not all the sobering facts! Every year some fifty-five thousand people die in alcohol-related auto crashes. In approximately half the murders in the country, either the killer or the victim—or both—had been drinking. Approximately a fourth of all suicides are found to have significant amounts of alcohol in their blood. It is said that people who abuse alcohol are *seven* times more likely to be divorced or separated than the general population, contributing to family instability. Forty percent of men admitted to mental hospitals are alcoholics.

The upswing in the use of alcohol is not just a US problem but a worldwide trend. France has the highest alcoholism rate, an estimated 10 percent to 12 percent of the population. And the Soviet Union may not be far behind, with "vodkaholics." In Italy and Israel drinking is an accepted social custom and there is little alcoholism. One researcher believes it is because, in these countries, drink is a happy companion to an occasion, not the occasion itself.

Some experts believe the problem is one of the destruction of traditional values and cite the example of the Eskimos and the American Indians. Dr. Charles Hudson, of the US Public Health Service in Alaska, says: "The major problem is one of social disintegration. The original social structure in rural Alaska has been blown apart . . . The things that were important to people have been taken away and when there's nothing to do, they'll take their last buck to get a bottle and stay drunk all the time."

The role of alcohol in American society has been distorted, confused, and riddled with vague and contradictory ideas. When you consider that approximately one hundred million Americans drink, it is truly amazing that so much misinformation exists on a subject of such obvious interest to so many. Two out of three Americans drink regularly and it is estimated that from 25 percent to 90 percent of young people, in selected areas, have used alcohol more than once. Many of those who don't drink pass harsh judgements on those who do. While shunning and condemning the alcoholic, many drinkers are uncritical of their own drinking habits.

When President Jimmy Carter on February 17, 1977, launched the nation's Committee on Mental Health, it was made plain that alcohol-related problems would be an important consideration. Mr. Carter spoke of the estimated cost to the nation of $37 billion from problems of mental illness, mental retardation, drug problems, emotional disturbances, and, last but not least, alcoholism. President Carter spoke of a number of private groups and government agencies in the health field which he felt should be "brought together." He said he hoped we have "torn down some of the tight walls that sometimes have been built around groups. . ."

Dr. Ernest P. Noble, director of The National Institute of Alcohol Abuse and Alcoholism, said: "The best hope of achieving any significant extension on life expectancy lies in the areas of alcohol abuse and alcoholism prevention."

With the ever-increasing air of controversy in the alcoholism treatment field, a "get tough" stance has more and more been urged from some traditional quarters. For example, a spokesman for The Council on Alcoholism for Northeastern Indiana (CANE) recently commented: "There's a rough, tough road to hoe in combatting alcoholism in Indiana and it's time we took off our gloves and got a little tough!"

Addressing an annual meeting of CANE, at Davis Ranch House, Richard Geizieichtner, assistant director of the Cooperative Extension Service at Purdue University, deplored the minimal funding devoted to fighting alcoholism in the state—and the so few effective treatment facilities. The speaker told his audience that "the best advice I ever received was, if you're going to accomplish anything, there's only one way—put your head down and butt!" Geizieichtner said: "You can be nice and pleasant and there's a time and place for that. But there is also a time for hard-knuckle fist fights!" He deplored the fact that there are people making important decisions "who don't know a thing about addictions. It's going to be a tough ballgame now," he said. The whole matter boils down to one of education, he believes, and he criticized the fact that many doctors as well as congressmen, "don't know a *damn* thing about it [alcoholism]—and its time they learned." Geizieichtner also urged that attempts be made only to implement "quality" alcohol programs and said the "homemade" variety would be too costly in terms of time and money.

In many states, highway safety programs have been set up with Drunk Driving Schools and a vast public campaign of education, stressing the alcohol toll in highway deaths. According to the president of the Licensed Beverage Industries, Inc., Thomas J. Donovan: "We are conscious that there exists in some quarters a bias against alcohol and drinking. Telling it like it is—whether we approve or disapprove—the majority of our population drinks. Attempts to distort highway safety efforts into a crusade against drinking generally will defeat the fundamental and basic purpose underlying effective public education programs."

Recently, Dr. Ernest Noble, Director of National Institute on Alcohol Abuse and Alcoholism has said: "In the past, we have looked at the individual. Now we are going to look at the agent." He asked for six research centers to be funded at $1 million each. Another trend today is to blame the media and advertising for the upswing in abusive drinking. Senator William Hathaway, chairman of the Senate Subcommittee on Alcoholism, not long ago raised the question of whether alcoholic beverages should be entirely banned from television, as a means of controlling the supply of alcohol. He also suggested adding additional taxes on all alcoholic beverages and raising the drinking age. The media also has been criticized for pictures showing President Jimmy Carter's brother with beer in hand. U.S. Senator Orin Hatch, calling Billy Carter a "folk hero," said: "I think he has a lot to say without opening a six-pack every time he comes on TV. I'd like to see some of the responsible leadership on TV act and moves be encouraged to keep the six-pack away from him until he's finished."

Taking the opposite view, Vincent T. Wasilewski, president of the Broadcaster's Association has said: "A ban on alcoholic beer advertising may further contribute to the 'forbidden fruit' image of alcohol, especially among the young." A spokesman for the Distilled Spirits Council of the U.S. (DISCUS) said: "Prohibitive taxes on alcohol will not be an effective solution to alcohol problems . . . realistic solutions will not come from *just* more money."

Thus, the "wet or dry" controversy is ageless and unresolved. With all the money spent, people are asking why alcoholism is still on the increase—almost to epidemic proportions, especially today among teens, older people, and women? Some members of the entrenched alcoholism establishment, as we have noted, blame the media for improper use of alcoholic beverages in films and on television. Others blame Women's Lib, economic stress, the increasing collapse of many American families, and political disenchantment. As alcohol authority A. Ludwig noted, at the Sixth Annual Alcohol Conference at Eaglesville, Pennsylvania: "The problems of the alcohol system will not be realized by having more money, more staff, and more facilities, but rather by qualitative changes in the nature of the activities conducted, a willingness to admit realistic scientific ignorance, and concerted efforts to remedy any of these deficits."

The problems of alcoholism are deeply rooted in our history, myth, and folklore. The disease concept did give the drunk a better deal by making him a patient rather than a criminal. It must be remembered that after World War II, two thirds of all arrests in major cities were for public intoxication. Today drunkenness is being decriminalized in most states. The disease idea saved the alcoholic from the "weak character stigma," and from that of "mental illness." But the popular view of alcoholism was created largely by laymen extolling white Protestant, middle-class values fashioned out of their own experiences.

What is happening today is that the shift from "you're not bad, you're sick" is being changed to "you're not bad *or* sick but doing inappropriate, self-defeating actions" calling for the use of behavior-modification techniques. In a sense, both the "bad" and "sick" labels are punitive. As long as we are a highly punitive society, some think deviance will prevail, with a high rate of both drug abuse and criminality. As a whole cannot reject its parts, so we cannot look on our drug abusers as if they were lepers, and not a part of us. As we look at the individual abuser, so also must we look at the system. In a report of the Fifth United Nations Congress, it was stated: "Combatting drug abuse itself might sometimes require changes in the social, economic, and cultural structure of a country in order to remove abuses and reasons for abusing drugs."

Why is our society still so uptight about drinking and drunks? Morris Chafetz, founding director of NIAAA, points out that "as a society, ours places a great deal of stock on order and control, and we find nothing more frustrating than watching somebody 'get away with' something. And we especially see it working against people who 'get away with' a loss of control, because of a severe alcohol problem. We become very retaliatory." And Junius Adams, author of *Drink to Your Health*, when asked in an interview if he thought our country was up tight about controls, answered: "Not about controls, but about controlling other people!"

When we consider that in our American society about 70 percent of the population drinks alcohol, either a lot or a little, we should come to realize that a black and white position is untenable. Alcohol has virtue as well as vice potential. Experts say that the percentage of total abstainers is on the decline. Drinking or not drinking, then, should be a personal choice of the responsible individual. We must avoid an extreme position. As Louis Pappalardo, bartender at the Waldorf Astoria Hotel in New York City observed: "There are millions of people in this country who are able to lead more cheerful, relaxed, and convivial lives because of liquor, and we shouldn't forget this fact." While alcohol abuse has always been a problem with men; today the men are being joined by women, teenagers, and older people.

According to a recent report, more members of elderly America are hitting the bottle. Dr. Frank Seixas, Medical Director of the National Council on Alcoholism, says: "There is not question that more old people are becoming alcoholics." He noted in an interview: "This could be due to our society's rejection of old people. There are fewer things a person is able to do, so he turns to the bottle." Other contributing factors can be soaring inflation, crowding in the cities, boredom, loneliness, fear, and worry. Dr. Seixas added: "Even though their financial resources may be shrinking, the temptation is to grab a bottle of liquor just to forget their problems."

Dr. George Brussel, a New York psychiatrist, believes older people are drinking more because they are dissatisfied with the present quality of life and doubt that it will improve. He says: "They are using drink to blot out things in an attempt to return to a past in which they felt more secure . . . Their drinking also results from economic hardships which are becoming worse. . . . I've been called in to see many more elderly patients, and I've seen many drunk in the streets."

Psychologically, some alcohol, in small amounts, can have a comforting effect upon the tired, the weary, and the aging. Two psychologists from the University of Massachusetts, Brian Mishara and Robert Kastenbaum, with two Harvard Medical School researchers, Frank Baker and Robert Patterson, did some research on using alcohol in a nursing home in the Boston area. Their study concluded that no adverse affects could be found and that there were some positive benefits.

Those nursing home residents who drank showed a decrease in worrying, had less trouble falling asleep, and showed an improved outlook on life. These patients also showed lower pulse rates which usually reflects better heart function. In addition, those who took part in the experiment tended to gossip less, to relate to others more congenially and intimately, and, as the experiment continued, began to ask for more responsibility in governing their own lives.

According to Dr. Joyce Brothers, some of the better, more progressive nursing homes are now introducing a social cocktail hour for patients. (Of course, if for no other reason than health and economics, the amounts are strictly limited.) She commented:

"This is one drug that, if used in moderation, can be helpful in making older people relax so they can enjoy themselves more and each other."

Dr. A. Aldama, of Mexico, was quoted in the ICAA News, the quarterly of alcoholism and drug dependence, as follows: "The use of alcohol and other drugs is *not* a medical problem, but rather a socio-economic one, or even a political problem. The individual and the society will not be able to liberate himself from alcohol or other drugs until he is liberated from inequitable power structures."

In a penetrating lecture, given in Spain in 1976, alcohol authority Dr. E. Bogani began by declaring himself a fatalist who could not see any simple solution to the problems of alcohol abuse, as "there is no way of separating the sociopathological factors from the entire socioeconomic context of society. In a life where there is no longer time to think, nor the inclination, but only time and desire to have pastimes that can be packaged and sold, a society is well on its way towards fatal aggression on the individual." He believes it is especially important to construct a society where the individual no longer needs to turn to drugs, any drugs, including alcohol.

Dr. Morris Chafetz, on the other hand, in his book on the historical importance of alcohol, *Liquor: The Servant of Man*, wrote: ". . . the desire for drink has been so keen, the quest for it so unremitting, and the use of it so continuous, that there can be little doubt about its importance to individuals and societies. There has always been—and always will be—a need for some agent by which man can alter his inner being in relationship to his environment." The problem, he feels, is not to do away with alcohol use, but only the abuse. And that's what *this* book is all about.

chapter 2

A Brief History of Alcohology

Alcohol is a part of our country's heritage and has always evoked strong emotion. From the beginning, there was a "wet or dry" controversy and it still continues today. Alcoholic beverages were brought to this country about 1607 with the settling of the Virginia Colony. Only a dozen years thereafter, the excessive use of alcohol resulted in a law decreeing punishment for offenders. The first time the drunk was privately reproved by his minister; the second time he was publicly rebuked, and the third time he was made to "lye in halter" for twelve hours and pay a fine. At the same time, the Virginia Assembly passed legislation encouraging the production of wines and spirits.

The first distillery was established on Staten Island in 1640 by William Kieft, a Hollander. Whiskey production became a way of life for many colonists. Like rum, brought in from the Caribbean, whiskey became a medium of exchange and barter. In the old days practically every farmer made whiskey. One famous farmer who became known for his distilling art was George Washington who, in 1761, ordered a still from England and began commercial production in 1762. A special area of his Mt. Vernon plantation was set aside to grow grain only for his distillery, which he named Dogue Run Farm.

The Whiskey Rebellion of 1794 was aroused by a federally imposed tax of seven cents on a gallon. George Washington himself put down the rebellion, but it took the action of fifteen thousand federal troops!

Some historians credit distillers with being a factor in the westward movement. Mennonite farmers, looking for a peaceful place to operate their stills, began to migrate west. Meanwhile, Puritans and others with a dark sense of sin and depravity, began loudly deploring drinkers as possessed by the devil. Drinking was related to immorality and the drinker was considered wicked and an object to be despised. He was ostracized or thrown in jail.

It was an Englishman, Thomas Trotter, who was the first doctor to argue for humane treatment of inebriates by placing them in special institutions. He called them "alcoholics" from the word *alcoholismus*, coined by Magnus Huss. The first such institute was the "House of the Fallen" opened in Boston in 1841 as a result of the efforts of Dr. Benjamin Rush (Dr. Trotter's American counterpart), who worked hard for better treatment for those with the disease of alcoholism in this country.

In the beginning, the disease concept was not popular with either the medical or lay people, as it was believed it gave the drunkard an excuse to drink. The Protestant ethic of hard work, thrift, and temperance was in full swing in America. The Temperance Movement was begun in the early 1800s, largely as a result of the Protestant view of walking the "straight and narrow path of righteousness." Actually, the *literal* meaning of temperance is moderate or controlled drinking; but gradually, as more voices were raised to say "drinking does more harm than good," it came to mean not drinking at all.

In 1919, the prohibitionists secured adoption of the Eighteenth Amendment to the U.S. Constitution, making it illegal to manufacture or sell any alcoholic beverages. The Woman's Christian Temperance Union had been formed in the early part of 1874 and, along with the Anti-Saloon League, begun in 1896, was a powerful prohibitionist force. The Anti-Saloon League, along with the Methodist Board of Morals, set up an office across the street from the White House and carried on one of the most vociferous and powerful of lobby demonstrations. Their efforts reached a peak of frenzy in World War I, even to the point of their linking the drinking of beer to venereal disease as part of their scare campaign to keep soldiers from drinking.

In 1917, the American Medical Association came out for prohibition. Woodrow Wilson, then President, was against prohibition, believing the states should decide for themselves. But against his wishes and that of a large part of urban America, the Eighteenth Amendment was passed. It was the Volstead Act which gave the Treasury Department the power to prosecute violations of the Amendment. But it received inadequate funds, was bothered by corruption of its own agents, and lacked public support. Fortunes were made in the bootleg liquor business. It was during this era that gangster mobs like the Mafia really got started and became big business. Gang wars were rampant! It was unsafe to walk to city streets!

A film called *Wet Vs. Dry* chronicles the "noble experiment" of Prohibition and shows how those who broke the law and drank became the "good guys", the socialities, the bootleggers, and the drinking public. Breaking the law became the acceptable way of life and much misunderstanding and confusion enveloped the use of alcohol. There still are highly confused attitudes that surround the use of spirits in our society today. (What is a prohibitionist? "A prohibitionist," quipped H.L. Mencken, "is the sort of man one wouldn't care to drink with—even if he drank!")

It is hard for us to understand how wild things were in those days when lawlessness often prevailed and many "decent people" were breaking the law. Crime increased everywhere, and gangsters operated openly. Al Capone and other gang lords had police protection. Much prohibition beer was brewed openly by farmers, who offered it for sale at roadside speakeasies. In 1925, New York boasted some thirty thousand speakeasies, as compared to fifteen thousand legal drinking places prior to prohibition. Prohibition wines were largely "dago red" and easy to get. In many cases illegal whiskey operations produced a dangerous rotgut. By 1930, at least fifty thousand Americans had been either blinded or killed by adulterated alcohol! Each year doctors wrote an average of 10 million prescriptions for alcohol "for medical reasons."

Prohibition finally had to be declared a distinct failure. It had only increased the public's desire for the "forbidden fruit." Economic pressure to revive the lucrative liquor industry also helped to repeal the Eighteenth Amendment. In 1933, the Senate voted to repeal the Amendment in all states. With drinking now legal, however, the country soon became a little too wet. Arrests for public intoxication soared. Jails quickly filled up with drunks. Soon new and forceful voices were raised saying these people were not sinful or willful, but victims of a strange and baffling new disease: alcoholism.

Dr. William Silkworth of Towns Hospital in New York declared, in the 1930s, that alcoholism was a "form of anaphylais." He believed that it resulted from an inborn allergy to alcohol that led inexorably to its abuse. One of Dr. Silkworth's patients was Bill W., cofounder of Alcoholics Anonymous (AA), in 1935. Long before the American Medical Association voted to recognize alcoholism as a disease in 1956, the disease concept was advanced by AA. (Originally, AA was part of a fundamentalist religious group, the Oxford Movement, whose membership included Bill W.)

Bill W., through the influence of Dr. Silkworth and the writings of William James, had come to believe he couldn't stay sober without getting religion. He had been impressed by a passage in James's *The Varieties of Religious Experience*: "The crisis of self-surrender is the throwing of our conscious selves at the mercy of powers, which whatever they may be, are more ideal than we are actually, and make for our redemption. Self-surrender has been and always must be regarded as the vital turning point of the religious life."

Impressed with the need for a religious life to keep himself sober, Bill W. had joined the Oxford group, which promised salvation through five life-changing stages. First a rapport was established between the "changer" and the "person to be changed." Confession was highly utilized. Efforts were made to achieve a "spiritual experience" and to follow God's teachings. After going through the five stages, the now "changed" person would find another "person to be changed" and thus make new converts for the group.

It is easy to see how these ideas came to be used in the confessional stories of AA, and how the "changer" became the AA sponsor. The five stages later became AA's "Twelve Steps" of recovery from alcoholism. Henry Tiebout, an early supporter of AA stated that the steps help induce the alcoholic to give up his inflated self-image in favor of God and the group. The alcoholic becomes as dependent on the group as he formerly had been on alcohol. Later AA played down its religious origins, admitting atheists and agnostics in order to get a wider following. With a five thousand dollar Rockefeller gift, AA soon got underway, literally sweeping drunks up off the city streets. (In those days, nobody wanted them anyway!) In a 1965 poll conducted by the National Council on Alcoholism, it was revealed that one third of all doctors polled, including psychiatrists, refused to treat alcoholics.[1]

The National Council on Alcoholism was founded in 1944 by a former AA member, Mrs. Marty Mann. The Council's activities, mostly referrals and public relations, are based on three concepts: (1) that alcoholism is a disease and that alcoholics are very sick people; (2) that alcoholics can be helped and are worth helping; (3) that alcoholism is a public health problem and a public responsibility. A public education program was begun that was enormously successful at asserting the disease concept.

Back in the 1930s, rather more quietly, behavioral science was also born. It began with aversive conditioning, a form of negative reinforcement. Investigators showed cards, for example, with liquor lables and simultaneously gave patients electric shocks. Films of alcoholics in delirium tremens or scary car wrecks were presented. Antabuse was given to alcoholics who were trying not to drink. (This substance would make a person violently ill if he or she took a drink.)

In the 1960s and 1970s, the trend has been to positive reinforcement, giving rewards for good behavior, such as, praise, token gifts, etc., rather than punishment for bad behavior. In the 1970s, therapists began to give assertiveness training, videotape confrontation, desensitization to stressful situations, and relaxation training. Family therapy was successfully introduced. Biofeedback was utilized to give information back to patients. A wide range of treatment modalities came into vogue, such as, psychodrama, yoga, transcendental meditation, and Zen. Perhaps the biggest and most controversial issue of the 1970s is controlled drinking vs. total abstinence for alcoholics. That battle still rages today.

In 1970, Congress approved the comprehensive Alcohol Abuse and Alcoholism Prevention Treatment and Rehabilitation Act, signed into law by President Richard Nixon. This made alcoholism a public health problem rather than a matter for the criminal justice system. The National Institute of Alcohol Abuse and Alcoholism was set up with Dr. Morris Chafetz as its first director. When asked in an interview, what was the first thing he was going to do, Chafetz said: "Get money. Money buys respectability!" NIAAA got money, lots of it. Journalist John Cashman wrote in his article, "Is Alcoholism a Myth?" (*Newsday*, September 28, 1975): "On the one hand it (NIAAA) supports the incurable but treatable-by-abstinence disease conception. On the other hand it has Congress to deal with in matters of funding. And Congress would like to know what it is getting for the taxpayer's money. It is called the cost-benefit ratio." Funding for all alcoholism programs rose from a meager amount in 1970, to more than four hundred six million dollars. In a budget request sent to Congress on February

22, 1977, President Carter asked for $153 million for NIAAA alone. Thomas J. Swafford, president of NCA, appeared before the Senate in April of 1977 advocating $225 million for NIAAA for the next fiscal year. "This is by no means a 'bare bones' or minimal request," he said. "But by no means is alcoholism a minute problem."

As a result of the rich funding of NIAAA, a new group of people became interested in alcohology: researchers, psychiatrists, psychologists, anthropologists, counselors, social workers, and scientists. Prior to NIAAA's founding in 1971, professional interest in alcoholism had been almost nil. Alcoholics had been mostly treated by lay people or recovered alcoholics and they prescribed that their charges think and act the same way they did in order to arrest their alcoholism. These converts were hostile to research, opposed to psychiatry, rigid in their thinking, and loyal to their own beliefs. As Dr. Linda Sobell of the Dede Wallace Center Alcohol Programs, Nashville Tenn. observed: "It is not surprising that persons who believe very deeply in traditional concepts . . . have known very few patients who contradicted their own beliefs."

In this regard, Morton S. Propper, famous alcohol expert, has noted: "If nonprofessionals suddenly stopped working with alcoholics, alcohol treatment programs would be brought to a halt." Because of the almost unchallenged power of AA in the treatment of alcoholism in the past forty years, laymen have become the uncontested "gatekeepers" of the wisdom of alcoholism treatment. Often these people are employed within the alcoholism establishment and their total abstinence is a condition of employment. This of course, gives them a vested interest in keeping the *status quo*. Moreover, if a person believes his sobriety and his job depend on his following the tenets of AA, he will not wish to hear about new treatment ideas, no matter how many drunks fall by the wayside and do not make it in the traditional program.

One researcher put it this way: "To hear of the success of others [doing moderate drinking] may be frustrating—and these workers prefer not to hear about it since it also upsets their treatment concepts . . . Granted that experimentation will yield discouraging relapses in most instances, this is not sufficient excuse for prejudiced persons to vilify the truth." Thus, the professional newcomer into the field is not too often warmly welcomed into the "house" of alcoholism treatment.

Despite much opposition, controlled drinking programs are here to stay; and I predict they will find greater and greater professional and public acceptance. Treatment programs of the future will move away from the medical, legal, and biological approach to alcoholism toward one more sociological, cultural, and anthropological. There will be a switch from imposing the will of the counselor on the alcoholic to trying to find out what the drinker wants to do in terms of wishing to abstain or merely to moderate a drinking habit. The counselor will help him or her to achieve that goal.

If the focus is just on stopping the drinking and not on the whole cluster of life problems surrounding the alcoholic, then he is sent back into the same environment with the same problems that originally drove him to drink. This is what creates "revolving door" alcoholics who keep coming back again and again for treatment. If the disease view is emphasized, public opinion and government policy tend to focus on the individual alcoholic as the source of the trouble.

However, if a "problems approach" is utilized, there will be a tendency to view the problems as directly related to interactions between the individual and his environment, and this will have profound implication for treatment and prevention programs.

One of the most promising areas for the study of alcoholism is in the sociological and cultural comparisons of the drinking practices and alcoholism ratios in different countries and cultures. This is aimed at finding out why alcoholism is higher in some countries or national, religious, and cultural groups than others. Interestingly, groups with a high rate of alcoholism include Irish Americans, northern Frenchmen, Americans, the Swiss, and northern Russians. Groups with a low incidence include Italians, Jews, Chinese, and Spaniards. It seems that those who use alcohol as part of a ritual or as a companion to food at the family table, such as the Italians, have fewer problems with alcoholism.

chapter 3

The Rand Report and the Alcohol War

When the prestigious Rand Corporation released, on July 10, 1976, a startling report suggesting that some alcoholics could safely return to social drinking, it was as if a bomb had exploded before the alcoholism establishment. The results of this report triggered an angry controversy that continues to this day. That this response was, and is, highly emotional is evidenced by such remarks as "many will die," "a blatant lie," and "cruel hoax." There were rumors that extraordinary efforts had been made to suppress the findings by very respectable people who don't ordinarily do that kind of thing.

The study was supported by a grant from The National Institute on Alcohol Abuse and Alcoholism (NIAAA), whose spokesmen still seem to find mention of the Rand report an embarrassment. They issue statements that are either highly defensive or acknowledge it only reluctantly, as a stepmother an unwanted child. The conclusions in the study came from research on 1,340 alcoholics treated in NIAAA-funded treatment centers in the U.S. At the start of treatment, the alcoholics were drinking nine times more alcohol than the average American, which was calculated at up to three ounces per day. These patients had shown serious behavioral and life adjustment problems. Over half had evidenced some kind of instability or lack of coping skills. At least half were unemployed, separated, or divorced. These volunteers took a variety of treatments including group and individual psychotherapy. After the followup, the report showed that the "relapse rate for normal drinkers was no higher than those who were long-range abstainers." Seventy percent showed substantial improvement. A third of the drinkers in the study abstained from alcohol for at least six months, a third drank normally, and a third drank heavily on occasion, but did abstain most of the time.

One of the strong points of the report was the number of people involved. The survey included some fourteen thousand clients based on treatment and intake followup data accumulated at forty-four alcoholism treatment centers throughout the U.S. Six months' followup was completed on 2,371 male clients. An eighteen month followup was completed on six hundred more male patients. Interviews, carried out up to eighteen months after treatment, showed that about 70 percent of the alcoholics had their drinking under control with no serious drinking consequences or symptoms. These alcoholics were doing the impossible: they were drinking "normally." On the average, their drinking consumption consisted of up to four cans of beer, four shots of liquor, or a pint of wine every three days.

Predictably, a patient with sound socioeconomic status had a better chance of recovery than others. An intriguing statistic was that formal treatment, of itself, adds no more than 20 percent to the recovery chances of the alcoholic. Remission of destructive drinking patterns was the "improvement criteria." The Rand Report was prepared by two prominent psychologists, David J. Armor and Harriet B. Stumbul, working with the well-known sociologist, J. Michael Polish. (The 215 page document is called *Alcoholism and Treatment* and is available for seven dollars from the Rand Corporation, Santa Monica, Ca. 90406.)

Actually, despite the ruckus it caused, the findings of the report are not earth shattering to the scientific community. A widely publicized study on controlled drinking was conducted in 1971 at Patton State Hospital, San Bernardino, Calif. This study asserted that controlled drinking is an effective treatment goal for certain kinds of alcoholics. In this study, ninety percent of the alcoholics were drinking moderately and functioning well after two years.

Indeed, there is a mass of previously ignored literature—at least sixty studies—on controlled drinking among alcoholics, dating back to the 1960s. David Armor commented on the finding that some alcoholics can drink normally by saying it is now "absolutely noncontroversial . . . at least, among the *research* community." One may wonder, *why*, then, did the headlines concerning the celebrated or infamous (depending on your point of view) report ignite such a controversy across the country? One observer feels that, for the first time, the deeply entrenched alcohol establishment felt challenged by the public reports of controlled drinking by alcoholics because they attacked its most fundamental belief.

Since it was brought directly to the attention of the general public by the popular press, it was experienced as a threat, not only to those sincerely protective of alcoholics, but to vast and far-reaching financial interests. Today alcoholism is big business, supplying many with well-paying jobs and providing generous research grants. Hospitals, through medical plans, are funded at an average of $120—$140 a day for the traditional two-week drying-out period, without having to provide *any* medical treatment. One formerly hospitalized alcoholic said, "I never saw a doctor, except passing in the halls! But they made me attend all those AA meetings." One doctor-director of a large metropolitan hospital confided to me at an alcoholism conference: "We've got to get the alcoholics to fill up the beds because people aren't getting sick as much and women aren't having as many babies." Even in some quarters where economics are not crucial to survival, the winds of change can be threatening.

While most critics of the Rand Report overwhelmingly evidenced true concern for the human values involved, as well as for the ideological implications, some overreacted almost to the point of hysteria. This reaction was possibly due to passionate conviction, a closed mind, or a dread of unwanted consequences. The "Alcohol War" was openly declared: Traditional alcohologists were allied solidly against the behavioral scientists and the researchers, and the puzzled public was in the middle wondering what all the fuss was about. Provocative questions were raised. Had alcoholism been a myth? Ideas that had been unchallenged for years were questioned by lay people and professionals alike.

Right after the report's publication, an army of clinicians, alcohologists, and researchers was assembled by the National Council on Alcoholism to assail the Rand Report and ridicule it as "unscientific," "shoddy," "dangerous dogma," and "a lousy piece of research." A reporter from *The New York Times* was amazed to discover that the NCA could hold a press conference to refute the study when from her questioning she discovered that not *one* spokesman at the conference had either seen or read it! Another reporter, after speaking with certain persons of the AA-NCA persuasion, complained of "the incredible closed mindedness, fanaticism, and paternalistic arrogance."

Dr. Nicholas Pace, president of the New York affiliate of NCA, was very angered by the report. He said: "A person cannot go back to controlled drinking when he has the disease of alcoholism. It is just not possible." He attacked the report for holding out "false hopes." He added: "You're going to see an awful lot of people die from the concept fostered by this report." NCA's medical director, Dr. Frank Seixas, accused the Rand authors of advancing a "startling and unethical proposal." Dr. Seixas, in what one imagines he took to be a parallel analogy, compared this to the US Public Health Service experiment in which patients with syphilis were maintained without treatment for a time to "study the course of the disease."

In Washington on July 1, 1976, twelve alcoholism authorities banded together to appear on a panel for a news conference called in response to the wide publicity given the Rand Report. Dr. Luther A. Cloud, NCA's vice chairman, said to the gathering at the Shoreham Americana Hotel: "Anything that gives [the alcoholic] a scientific excuse for drinking is a matter of concern to us." He noted that in New York City there were reports of alcoholics dropping out of treatment. Dr. Cloud deplored the fact that the study had not been submitted, before release, to "peer review." Rand researcher David Armor defended the release of the report. "It was an appropriate time to release it," he told a reporter from *Behavior Today* magazine.

It should be mentioned that the authors of the Rand Report had been quick to caution that there are as yet no criteria for identifying those alcoholics who can return to normal drinking and those who cannot. They further warned that those with liver disease or other alcohol-related physical complications, shouldn't try to drink *at all*, nor should those who have tried to moderate and failed. (Little note was paid to these cautions.)

Dr. Joichi Takamine, chairman of the American Medical Association's Committee on Alcoholism, said he feared the report "will create havoc in the homes of alcoholics and carnage on the highways." He declared, "Abstinence is the *only* way for an alcoholic to stay healthy." Another outspoken foe of the report was Dr. Mary Pendery, a San Diego, California, authority on alcoholism and head of the State Advisory Board. She criticized the researchers for relying on alcoholics for information as to whether or not they were drinking and how much in followup studies. She called the researchers "naive" to believe the word of alcoholics, who, she said, are "notoriously unreliable." An AA spokesman exclaimed: "They were relying on the statements of alcoholics and in our judgment they are the biggest liars in the world." A Rand spokesman asserted that findings were not based on an alcoholic's single response to a question, but rather to his answers to multiple questions, so that the answers could be examined for consistency.

While NCA spokesmen denied that any attempt was made to suppress the findings of the report, evidence points to the contrary. Dr. Pendery took angry issue with the way the report was released. She said: "One of the most disheartening episodes of this entire fiasco was the unbending refusal of Gustav Shubert (a senior vice-president of Rand) to delay release of the final version for even a few days to permit top scientists, who were standing by, to meet with him . . . to provide detailed documentation of the shortcomings of the report and its inevitable, tragic consequences." Dr. Pendery, who had done her homework and actually read the Rand Report, called it "a case built on cotton candy." She told a reporter: "I, myself actually called him [Shubert] at home, at breakfast, in a last attempt to persuade him to hold such a meeting." But Mr. Shubert refused to delay release of the findings—to the applause of some and the horror of others. In rebuttal, Dr. Pendery called the Rand Corporation's conduct "a violation of scientific ethics." (Researcher Armor later wrote off Dr. Pendery as "someone who doesn't care what the data say.")

A spokesman for the Rand people asserted that it would have been "absurd" to withhold publication just because the conclusions were "counter intuitive." He affirmed that the findings had been carefully checked and rechecked by sources both within and without the company. It later came out that a month before the report was published, former Senator Harold Hughes and Senator William Hathaway, chairman of the Senate Subcommittee on Alcoholism, had met to explore legal ways of delaying the release of the report to the public. Morris Chafetz admitted that he had been under heavy pressure to suppress the report when an earlier version had been produced a year before. Rumors circulated that Thomas Pike, a Los Angeles industrialist and long-time activist in alcohol-rehabilitation programs and a member of the Rand Corporation, had tried unsuccessfully to get the report killed. A "recovered" alcoholic himself, Pike has since resigned as a member of the board at Rand in protest. Pike called the work "bum statistics" and spent a year or so trying "to get them (the researchers) on the right track." Another critic called it "propaganda for death."

On an NBC-TV program, *The Tomorrow Show*, July 8, 1976, Harriet Stumbel defended the report, affirming that some alcoholics definitely can drink again. She reiterated: "There are more than sixty studies over the past twenty-five years which carefully report this same phenomena." She noted that while numerous experiments had been begun to prove that one drink can set up the uncontrollable compulsion to drink, no one in the scientific community has come up with any proof whatsoever. She believes that in alcoholism treatment there should be considered more "flexible goals" than total abstinence for some alcoholics. "When control is not thought possible, no attempt is made to achieve it," she commented. "If you fall off the wagon and have one drink, you are going to tell yourself you might as well go ahead and have ten." Both Chafetz and Ms. Stambul believe that the idea—if you pick up one drink, you'll go crazy and won't be able to stop—could become a "self-fulfilling prophesy."

In an editorial titled "One Drink Is Still Too Many" the Tacoma, Washington, *News-Tribune* had written: "To control the disease, simply give up alcohol—forever! The eighteen months spent on the Rand Report would have been better spent discovering how many fleas can perch on the head of a pin! Indeed, even that would have made more sense!" In a news item in the *Los Angeles Times* on June 12, 1976, California members of the Alcoholism Advisory Board, who met in San Francisco, were quoted as calling the Rand Report "methodologically unsound and clinically unsubstantiated. The lives of many persons with the disease are now endangered." But Dr. Robert Moore, a San Diego, California, physician and researcher, says he found the study was "carried out in a reasonable manner" and that the critics were merely "nitpickers." (One wonders whether the Rand people could have produced *any* report that the alcoholism establishment would have accepted, given the findings.) Defenders of the report called the critics' attitude "ugly paternalism."

When a reporter asked Dr. Cloud why Ernest P. Noble, current NIAAA director, had not immediately repudiated the report if it was such an "amateurish work" and so "seriously flawed," Cloud remarked that Dr. Noble had "inherited a very smelly kettle of fish when he succeeded Chafetz as director of NIAAA." Dr. Noble was not long silent, and on June 23, 1976, he released a statement saying that "until hard evidence is produced to the contrary, abstinence must continue as the appropriate goal in the treatment of alcoholism." (It was not defined what Dr. Noble considered "hard evidence.") He told Congress he was dismayed by the way in which the report was released to the news media, prior to further scientific scrutiny, and promised to keep a "careful eye" that such "goings-on" would not happen in the future. A Congressman told Dr. Noble that the report had caused an enormous furor, adding that he hoped that "something would be learned from this, so that in the future, these grants would have "a few conditions attached." He added: "After all, three hundred thousand dollars is not a bad deal for them [the Rand people]. They should be willing to cooperate a bit."

Representative Wilbur Mills, breaking AA anonymity at 'the public level against AA policy, had come forth and claimed a cure for his own alcoholism, which had formerly gotten him into trouble with an attractive stripper and caused scandal and embarrassment. He made a statement that Congress should take responsibility to see that "money made available through the federal government for alcohol abuse and alcoholism studies is properly used and awarded for scientific studies that will be helpful and not harmful to alcoholics." (This is contrary to scientific methodology, which affirms that the results of tests should be not *pre*determined, but rather based on scientific findings.)

The NCA distributed a paper with the blaring headline: "Alcoholics Fail to Control Drinking," which told of a study made by Dr. John A. Ewing, director of the Center for Alcohol Studies at the University of North Carolina in 1975, in which *no* successes were reported. Traditionalists have called it "the definitive study on controlled drinking," but Ewing, himself, called it "strictly a pilot study." He had assembled thirty-five alcoholics who had rejected AA and chose to try controlled drinking. After the first meeting, ten dropped out; and after a few more, eleven fell by the wayside, leaving only fourteen to master the art of moderate drinking. In a follow-up, all but possibly one had returned to their old abusive habits. A common complaint was that controlled drinking is more difficult than abstinence. (But difficult is not the same as impossible.)

The ripple effect of the Rand Report continued stirring up other quarters. Under the heading "Report Enrages Ex-alcoholic," Ann Landers printed a reader's letter complaining that the statement that some alcoholics can drink again was "tantamount to tossing a firebomb into a crowd at a football stadium." The irate reader went on to say: "Rand deserves a kick in the collective pants for their irresponsibility in releasing such destructive materials." Ann Landers was "horror-struck" by the Rand release and added: "I hope that enough high-powered experts in the field of alcoholism will clobber that report sufficiently so that we will soon be reading a retraction." She blasted the report as being "idiotic and dangerous!"

But, as writer Sandy Hotchkiss observed in an article on the Rand Report that appeared in a Washington paper: "What the assailants of the study fail to realize is that the heated criticism of the report caused by their violent denunciations were serving less to protect the vulnerable alcoholic, than to keep the issue in the forefront, where misunderstandings could most likely do the most damage."

Thus the "Alcohol War" which had broken out over the Rand Report continues, and is not quick to subside, even as the flurry of media coverage of the report dies down. Not long after, the authoritative and widely honored Rutger's *Journal of Studies on Alcohol* ran several articles that hurled more fuel on the flaming controversy which again were widely publicized by networks and media people for they had found the subject was "hot." The public wanted to read about the controversy. One such article solidly supporting the Rand Report was written by Doctors Ovide Pomerleau, Michael Pertschuk, and James Stinett, researchers at the University of Pennsylvania. They came forth boldly to assert that alcoholism is not an irreversible, physical disease which prevents all its victims from ever safely picking up a drink. They pointed out that this widespread belief (fostered by AA/NCA people in their propaganda) was based on a "working hypothesis" of the late E.M. Jellinek and is entirely unproven and, in fact, evidence exists to the contrary.

Another article in the Rutger's *Journal* told of a study made by the Addiction Research Foundation of Ontario, Canada, where ninety-six alcoholics were given a four-week treatment program and the goal was moderation. The follow-up a year later showed that eighteen, or about 20 percent, were drinking in a controlled manner (defined as drinking small quantities of alcohol only occasionally and not having any alcohol-related problems).

Morris Chafetz spoke up: "The field of alcoholism should be overjoyed by the Rand Report." He added: "What it does is to show that alcoholism is a very treatable disease." In an article in the *New York Times* on the report Chafetz was quoted as saying that the "present rigid, stereotypic thinking" about alcoholism could be "self-defeating." "For a person who lives in a drinking society to think he must stop drinking entirely to control his alcohol problem, may discourage him from seeking treatment until he's really down in the dumps . . . and when total abstention is the only definition for recovery from alcoholism, the alcoholic who takes his *first* drink is labeled a failure—and this, in itself, may cause him to go on a binge."

On a television program called *Crossfire*, aired in Washington, D.C. on July 19, 1976, he pointed out the amazing recovery rate of 70 percent evidenced by some alcoholics in the report but painfully acknowledged that he felt there was an "implicit lack of respect in this country for alcoholic people, even found in people who treat alcoholics."

He noted: "they wanted this report suppressed" because of what he termed the "chance findings" of the report. Chafetz said: "They keep saying that alcoholics will start to drink because of this report and it should be kept from them, as though they were children who must be protected against truthful, scientific information." He said there was a further implication that alcoholics were really considered "weak-willed people," who, because a report said some alcoholics could drink again, would all "run out and do it." (He has recently written a book called *Why Drinking Can Be Good for You.*)

Both he and others on the show said they hoped the Rand Report would cause traditionalists to rethink or, at least, reexamine some of the dogma now treated as gospel by the majority of the alcoholism establishment, referring presumably to the one treatment (abstinence) syndrome prevalent in the field for forty years. Meanwhile, back at the Rand Corporation's California headquarters, the "much ado" about the report had generated a controversy unprecedented in the firm's distinguished history. It had long been noted for painstaking scientific studies and quiet domestic research; and it prized its reputation for integrity.

Their report, however, had given the alcoholism community a "rude shock" and the repercussions seem endless. For the hard-rock edifice of traditional alcoholism treatment has been built on such rigid dogma as the necessity for total abstinence and the idea that what is good for *one* alcoholic, is good for *all*. (In AA they are fond of saying: "Do you think you're *special*?") Most unbiased, rational thinkers, however, find that while the Rand Report may be lacking the ultimate in methodology, it is a very substantial piece of work and will continue to have an important impact on the field of alcoholism treatment for many years to come. As Chafetz commented: "The field of alcoholism doesn't have *all* the answers. What's wrong with questioning some of the conventional wisdom?" (What's wrong, indeed?!)

"If we are really committed to helping alcoholic people, there is no danger in keeping an open mind about the nature of the problem," says Chafetz. "Since some sixty studies indicate that a percentage of recovered alcoholics are at this moment social drinkers (I know several devoted members of AA who drink moderately), we ought to ask whether demands for total abstinence are not too harsh and unrealistic. Indeed, they may even cause people who need moderate amounts of alcohol in their lives to avoid treatment until late in their illness."

In his opinion, the professional alcoholism establishment's overreaction to the Rand Report will not prevent alcoholic people from recovering. But he says, "The paternalistic attempt to protect alcoholics from themselves by suppressing the study's conclusions is a gesture of profound contempt that only increases the social stigma alcoholics have experienced for far too long."

chapter 4

Trying to Recover
from the Disease Concept

When continued overdrinking passed from the "sin" category to that of a "disease," it was considered a scientific victory. Today the whole disease concept is under fire, especially by researchers in the social sciences. Dr. M. M. Glan of Britain says it is a semantic problem based on your definition of a disease. One researcher has written a paper cleverly called: "Defining Alcoholism: the Alcoholist's Disease."

But semantics can be crucial, when from them pours the lavish cup of awarded (or withdrawn) financial support as well as dictating policies of prevention, diagnosis, and treatment. Chafetz and others have pointed out that alcoholism is a function of social perception, dependent both upon a personal evaluation and a cultural bias. In one study doctors tended, for example, to designate a patient an alcoholic if he was *not* working. If the patient was economically advantaged (gainfully employed), they would elect some physical diagnosis for the problem, such as liver trouble, and avoid the "alcoholic" label. One wit says the alcoholic is the person who stops bragging and starts lying about his drinking.

Dr. Jerome Geisler, of the Alcohol Program of Roosevelt Hospital in New York, says: "Quite simply, the alcoholic is the guy that can't make it home to Westport without the club car. He's the guy who can't take alcohol and leave it—he has to take it!" Actually, as Chafetz has pointed out, all illness is socioculturally determined. There is no biologically labeled illness. Illness is what we make it. "Disease is what the medical profession labels as such," said Dr. Jellinek. Problem drinking or alcoholism can be put under the umbrella of "maladaptive use of alcohol." Jellinek's definition was: "any use of alcoholic beverages that causes damage to the individual or society or both." (It was vague by design.)

34

What is a disease? The word *disease* comes from the Latin *dis* meaning "lack," and *ease*, meaning "freedom from pain." Thus, in its simplest form, disease means dis-ease. The *Random House Dictionary* describes it as: "A condition of an organ, part, structure, or system of the body in which there is incorrect function, resulting from the effects of heredity, infection, diet, or environment." *Stedman's Medical Dictionary* speaks of disease primarily in terms of "microorganismal alteration."

In 1954, the World Health Organization defined alcoholism as a "chronic behavioral disorder manifested by repeated drinking of alcoholic beverages in excess of the dietary and social uses of the community and to an extent that it interferes with the drinker's health, or his social, or economic functions." The American Psychiatric Association's diagnosis of alcoholism is: "for patients whose intake of alcohol is great enough to damage their personal health or their personal or social functioning, or when it has become a prerequisite to normal functioning."

Some medical men as well as lay persons have difficulty accepting alcoholism as a disease, in the sense of cancer, TB, or measles. A loose definition given is "any deviation from health." According to Mrs. Marty Mann, author of *The New Primer on Alcoholism*: "Alcoholism is a disease which manifests itself chiefly by the uncontrollable drinking of the victim, who is known as an 'alcoholic'. It is a progressive disease. . .which has only two outlets: insanity or death." Are we to assume then, if this dogmatic statement is correct, that if an overdrinker can control his drinking, that he is not an alcoholic? Recovery in terms of moderation must be considered a possibility, as research affirms.

Considerable amounts of literature have been distributed with the idea of educating the general public to the fact that overdrinking is a medical and not a criminal problem by such organizations as the National Council on Alcoholism and the US Public Health Service. It's true, of course, that chronically taken, large amounts of alcohol can have a pathological effect on the human organism, just as taking an inordinate amount of aspirin over a long time is also detrimental to the human body. (Dr. Mortimer Hartman, Medical Director of Drink Watchers reported a patient addicted to aspirin.) Nonetheless, we do not have a disease labeled 'aspirholism' with its victim labeled 'aspirholic'. Dr. Thomas Szasz of the State University of New York points out that prior to labeling hysteria a disease, it was regarded as malingering, and physicians refused to pay any heed to it, until it was accepted as a mental illness. As Drs. Linda and Mark Sobell, alcohol scientists, have noted: "there are two consequences of labeling, which may serve to 'lock-in' the deviant behavior. The first is the process of rejecting the individual from the primary group, which evidences intolerance of his drinking. The second consequence of labeling may be the functional integration of the labeled individual into social groups which are composed mainly of nondeviants. Potentially unstable families or friendship groups may be stabilized by the presence of the deviant."

The function of the deviant's presence may be to define *other* members of the group as "healthy" or "normal", the presence of a submissive target for scapegoating, or an excuse for the lack of goal achievement of the group. As Drs. Mark and Linda Sobell put it, "The disease label has disease consequences," as a result of assigning to the patient a specific role and with it the role expectations.

Problem drinking or alcoholism, it has been pointed out by *Newsday* journalist John Cashman, is the only disease where medical men will refer you to a pseudoreligious organization for healing with words alone. Moreover, it is the only disease where the patient's symptom is forbidden. Actually, alcoholics had been forsaken by medical men until the behavioral scientists, interested in behavior modification techniques, embraced the "still-suffering alcoholic," hoping, and often with much success, to return him successfully to social drinking.

Alcohol researcher Professor W. Feuerlein of Germany notes that the "principal difficulty in the diagnosis of alcoholism resides in the fact that, like schizophrenia, it [alcoholism] leaves no traces that can be revealed by blood tests or x-rays; the symptoms are diffused throughout the medical, psychological, and social spheres of reference."

Mrs. Fred Tooze, when head of the National Women's Christian Temperance Union, defined an alcoholic as *"anyone who drinks alcohol.* As soon as they start to drink, they're on that road downhill," she said. But, as Morris Chafetz observed, "You don't have to drink to have a problem with alcohol. I think Carry Nation was an alcoholic—a *non-drink*ing alcoholic. She couldn't take care of her children, couldn't live with her husband, because she was so obsessed with Demon Rum. Didn't she have a problem with alcohol?"

There was a David Susskind television show with five alcoholism experts bogged down for two and a half hours trying to define alcoholism. The problem is there is no fundamental agreement on definitions of alcoholism or alcoholism recovery. The very word alcoholic is loaded with superstition, prejudice, and myth. Is an alcoholic defined by the *amount* consumed or the *effect* of alcohol on his person or his life? How about recovery? Should that be in terms of total abstinence, controlled drinking, or viewing alcohol use as only part of successful life adaptation?

Defining alcoholism as a disease has prescriptive implications. What happens when you are ill? The doctor gives you some pills and you get better. In fact, it can be argued that the mere referral to a physician is a form of labeling. (Person can't help himself—needs professional help). Thus the stage is set for progression, by assigning the sick role to the person. Pressure, through constructive coercion, will be brought to bear upon the deviant, usually through the "significant others" in his life: mate, relatives, employers, who will be asked to take a "get tough" policy. The employer now has an excuse to fire him at any sign of absenteeism or slackening of work skills. It should be noted that the employer rarely needs to know more about the condition than that the person "drinks," for the employer to assume that he is also irresponsible, untrustworthy, or immoral.

The assignment of the disease label is also bad for the individual's self-concept. On the one hand, he is told that he is sick and, on the other hand, he is told to "shape-up" and above all stop drinking. He may make extraordinary efforts to do this. Or he may fall by the wayside. (One such man who got drunk was asked why he did it, to which he replied: "This is what alcoholics do, they drink.") Since the disease is said to be terminal, progressive, and incurable, what chance does he have to fight it? He may find it easier to carry out the deviant's role than to make the giant character changes said to be necessary to have a spiritual awakening and lose the urge to drink. For the rest of his life, if he chooses to "shape-up", he must give top priority in his life to only one thing: staying away from one drink, one day at a time. Everything else must fall in place around this central idea: vocation, family, friends, and even geographic location.

The researchers Gerard, Wile, and Saenger found in evaluating a group of abstinent "successes" that 43 percent were conspicuously disturbed; 24 percent inconspicuously inadequate; 12 percent AA successes, and 10 percent independent successes. The point made was that for some people a moderate amount of alcohol has a normalizing effect on personality function which, if totally removed, may lead to deterioration of one's coping capacity. The idea that total abstinence can have a "personality price" has not been a consideration in the past by workers in the field.

Researchers have pointed out that abstinence, in terms of overall life adaptation, may be followed by deterioration in total life health. An obvious example is the borderline psychotic who uses alcohol to ally anxiety or to maintain ego integration and who becomes psychotic when totally removed from alcohol. Thus abstinence and mental health are not necessarily related, although they could be with some drinkers.

There are medical consequences of drinking to excess, to be sure, which may even follow a predictable course. But the disease model of alcoholism has some very unfortunate limitations. It gives the incorrect impression that the doctor alone can deal with the cause and treatment of alcoholism. It identifies the client as a patient in need of treatment, often removing him from family and job and isolating him from his everyday places and problems. It emphasizes the helplessness of the person rather than his degree of self-determinism. It completely rules out the importance of environmental, cultural, and economic factors. It provides the drinker with an excuse or alibi for not changing his behavior. If the overdrinker already suffers from low self-esteem, labeling him an alcoholic will only add to his poor self-image. If he is made to feel guilty, this will only heighten his already overwhelming problems. He may become a kind of "moral leper" to his normal associates. On the one hand, he is told that he has a disease, and there is no moral culpability for acts done while under the influence. On the other hand, in AA facilities, he is told he must make amends for wrongs previously done. As long as the disease concept prevails, a person cannot get help for a drinking problem without the fanfare of the "Return of the Prodigal Son."

Labeling persons as deviants merely perpetuates deviance. These people will then join deviant groups and become even more alienated from the mainstream of society. It contributes to the idea that there exists two kinds of drinkers: alcoholics and normal people. It does not define them by their actions, which could be interchangeable. A normal person could at some time drink heavily and an alcoholic could drink moderately. It rather describes the alcoholic intrinsically as a metabolic cripple born with a tragic flaw in his makeup that can never be corrected. He is alleged to be a person of permanent physiological abnormality. In the ultimate cop-out, AA people say if an alcoholic does learn to moderate his drinking habits, it merely proves he never was an alcoholic in the first place!

There is, especially, on the part of the alcoholism establishment and, strangely enough, in reformed drunks or recovered alcoholics a very moralistic attitude toward the alcoholic. Possibly because it is threatening to them to see someone out of control, as it becomes a mirror of their own weakness. They develop a very judgmental and vindictive attitude toward alcoholic people. In many areas, alcoholism is grounds for divorce and loss of driver's license. The alcoholic person may not hold public office, and alcoholism is a basis for job discrimination.

In this regard, Dr. Morris Chafetz wrote: "I am struck by the fact that such moralism is not only seen in the general public but is highlighted in physicians and—some would say oddly—in many recovered alcoholics. By and large both groups, though they make a pose of caring, really offer a terrible put-down to people who abuse alcohol. This attitude shows itself in a number of ways: (1) paternalism or talking down to (2) impossible standards of recovery (no drink ever, so that failure is almost guaranteed) and (3) a kind of therapeutic nihilism (diagnosis and treatment are both hard to get). At almost every level of society, there is a negative feeling for people, who, we feel, are having a good time losing control with alcohol, while we have to behave ourselves.

"Nothing, of course, could be further from the truth, because alcoholic people don't really enjoy alcohol. It is an anesthetic drug—and a very good one at that—and deadens whatever pains them from whatever sources that afflict them. The society that screams at them, judges them, preaches at them, and laments them seems not to understand how desperate a person must be to choose, if indeed he does choose, an illness so despised by the rest of us."

Dr. Richard Shore, former Director of the City Health Department's Bureau on Alcoholism in San Francisco, Calif., stated in an interview: "Many alcoholics may respond better to modified or controlled drinking than to total abstinence . . . the disease concept is tied to abstinence and pictures the alcoholic as passive and dependent . . . and when you try to sell this to a middle-class American, he will say, 'I'm not an alcoholic'!"

According to Mark and Linda Sobell ". . .it is possible for an alcoholic to become totally abstinent with regard to alcohol, but to simultaneously manifest a psychotic condition or poor social functioning." Mark Keller, editor of the *Journal of Studies on Alcohol*, has stated: "The therapeutic goal of permanent abstinence may be too extreme for all cases; many long-confirmed alcoholics cannot achieve it, and more moderate features of improvement, reduced frequency of intoxication, and reduced duration of drinking bouts are valid gains."

Dr. E. Mansell Pattison says that "in a significant portion of treated alcoholics, improvement in drinking skills and improvement in social, vocational, and psychological adaptation are related, but not parallel." He believes: "less than total rehabilitation" may be the most feasible therapeutic goal in many cases. He adds further "that abstinence is misleading as a criterion of successful treatment; and moreover, it may be maintained only at the expense of total life functioning, as in some AA abstainers." Abstinence may be followed by personality deterioration, the switching of symptoms to another problem such as hypochondria, depression, under-achieving and a variety of mental illnesses and personality disorders.

The disease concept contributes to the idea that treatment efforts need be only directed at the alcoholic himself. It also gives the impression that the medical professional is the only help needed, when there may well be a need for finding help in preparing for a vocation, or further education, more meaningful structuring of free time, and guidance in personal relations. Thus, the problem could require the help of social workers, pastoral counselors, educators, psychologists, etc., in addition to that of a doctor.

The illness model has been called counterproductive because it fails to incorporate phenomena that are properties of social collectives and it makes no allowances for cultural differences. According to Dr. Donald Finlay of the University of British Columbia: "My own appraisal of recent research in this area suggests that counselors who have a family interactional conception of alcohol problems are more effective than those who operate out of the traditional illness framework."

As Dr. Finlay has written: "In short, labeling an alcohol dependent person as 'sick' hinders more than it helps the efforts of both the business community and professionals who would, could, or might be of assistance, for the illness concept of alcoholism makes people at all levels and in all capacities very uncomfortable about applying pressure that works—or sustaining the response that such pressure engenders . . . To paraphrase, how can you do that (apply pressure) to a sick person, who, by definition, has lost control over his drinking and cannot be held responsible for being sick? The final effect of the illness model is thus to minimize the element of choice which people who overly rely on alcohol are able to exercise and which they generally do exercise when they know in clear, concrete, and highly visible ways, 'what's in it for them'."

It was Dr. E.M. Jellinek's disease model (seized upon by AA with great gusto) which gave rise to the public's idea that alcoholism is a disease of deadly progression. But even in his original article, Jellinek maintained that some people get "stuck" at one stage or another. Jellinek spoke of the loss-of-control which occurs in only two groups of alcoholics and then only after many years of excessive drinking. He concluded in his book, *The Disease Concept of Alcoholism* (1960), that "only *gamma* and *delta* alcoholisms qualify as diseases, because only they are addictions in the pharmacological sense."

In Jellinek's five types of what he preferred to call "alcoholisms," he denoted *gamma* as the most prevalent in the US, the AA type. He defined this type as having increased tissue tolerance to alcohol, withdrawal symptoms, cravings, and loss-of-control. *Delta* he described as having the same characteristics, except for "loss-of-control" he substituted "inability-to-abstain." He also defined the two types which he considered not to be a disease: *alpha* which he characterized as simple, continued use of alcohol to relieve emotional or physical pain, with any dependence being purely psychological in nature and with the drinking resulting in no serious consequences. *Beta* was characterized by physical complications resulting from over use of alcohol but had neither physical nor psychological dependence. *Episilon* was less clearly defined, except as a form of periodic addiction. He emphasized that the listing of only five types of "alcoholisms" was by no means exhaustive and that all they each had in common was a maladaptive use of alcohol.

Jellinek also wrote that "there is every reason why the student of alcoholism should emancipate himself from accepting the exclusiveness of the picture of alcoholism as propounded by Alcoholics Anonymous." But who ever hears this in the field?

Another popular misconception concerns researcher Tiebout's concept of "hitting bottom," which was taken to mean, by workers in the field, that all treatment is futile until the alcoholic hits his nadir (has gotten enough *hell*) to make him surrender to treatment and, most of all, to total abstinence. To facilitate this, giving alcoholics a little push in the form of threatened loss of job, spouse, children, etc. (which may actually be carried out) can be rationalized. This is called "constructive coercion" or "crises intervention." It stated in one NIAAA booklet that the hospital should be the "point of attack" on the alcoholic. (Intoxicated persons are often brought in against their will by police for involuntary commitments.) In fact, the AA model can lead to such over-zealousness that the person's civil liberties are violated.

Persons in need of treatment are usually people in trouble of some sort, either financially, legally, or emotionally. They can be easily coerced into making rash commitments. The pressure may be internal, external, or both, to "do something" about the problem. Yet, most often they will not be placed in a position of free choice. (And when you make a bargain from a position of weakness, when you get strong again, as you will, you will resent the bargain made in weakness.) This is somewhat the position of many persons forced into abstinence programs and also explains why there is such a high dropout rate.

For some drinkers, obviously, there is a strong need and desire for a chemical comforter to insulate themselves from what's bothering them in their world. And it is nonsense to believe they will give up so easily a substance that they feel has, in the past, brought them such exquisite relief. To expect them to stop drinking and have a sudden character change is unrealistic. Character change takes a lot of time and work: trust-building, creating good relationships, etc. Wouldn't it make more sense to let some of these overdrinkers at least try to moderate their drinking before con-demning them to a life of abstinence?

One researcher criticized total abstinence as the sole treatment goal on several grounds: (1) poor results, (2) unusual quality of medical care, and (3) the inhibition of development of different treatments based on other aims. He noted: "It is becoming in-creasingly difficult to defend total abstinence as the exclusive aim of the treatment of alcoholics". Also abstinence requires lifelong treatment to sustain.

Researchers Gillis and Kent (1969) have provided the scientific world with evidence that abstinence, per se, is not necessarily synonymous with improved psychological adjustment—only ap-proximately 10 percent of the totally abstinent patients they studied were psychologically stable: a disturbing number were found to have increased pathology. Other researchers have sug-gested that abstinence, as a treatment goal, may be enormously difficult to maintain and may actually place the alcoholic under a tremendous strain.

Yet, the NCA issued a press release (1974) stating: "There have been some claims that alcoholics can drink again. We view these as misleading and dangerous . . . Abstinence from alcohol is necessary for recovery from alcoholism . . . There is a need for responsible research, carried out with controls, as well as judicious publication of results when pertinent . . . However, we believe . . . no alcoholic may return with safety to any use of alcohol."

As Linda Sobell has noted: "the use of the word "*judicious*" seems, in fact, intended to discourage scientists from pursuing investigations of whether or not alcoholics can successfully moderate their drinking; (we are aware of no *injudicious* publication of results of scientific studies)!" She says: "There are two grave dangers from this statement. The first concerns a significant threat to freedom of scientific inquiry. The question of whether some alcoholics are capable of resuming drinking is hardly heuristic and for that matter, has already been answered. The second danger is more imminent and concerns what Dr. Morris Chafetz has characterized as a "paternalistic" attitude towards the alcoholic among workers in the alcoholism field. This attitude can best be summarized as 'I know what's best for them' or 'they are poor misguided souls'.

She further notes that it is indeed paradoxical and ironic that those individuals who most loudly proclaim that one of their major objectives is to remove the moral stigma which considers alcoholism to be symptomatic of a 'weak willpower' or a 'weak personality' are the ones who would not trust the alcoholic to have access to the facts about his disorder.

John Cashman writing in his brilliant article, "And Never a Drop to Drink?" (*Newsday*, June 23, 1976), has commented: "As always when faced with conflicting information, the orthodox alcohologists circle their idealogical wagons and begin firing blindly at the savage researchers." John Cashman points out: "The field of alcoholism is such a monument to frustration that any new insights or innovative approaches to the problem would be expected to be more than welcome. Paradoxically, the opposite is true.

"At issue," he says, "is the difference between dogma and the establishment of scientific fact. They are not often compatible approaches to the quest for truth. And the point is that in the field of alcoholism, the dogmatic has the upper hand. The proof of this is the inability of the majority of workers in the field to see beyond their own beliefs . . . Dogmatism has a totalitarian aversion to anything but revealed truth. The faithful believe, the infidels are made to suffer . . . Statistics indicate that there are 9 million alcoholics who have not yet been converted to the doctrinaire wisdom of the true believers. You would think that the alcohol establishment would be more interested in helping them than in perpetuating precious dogma. Given the evidence, you would be wrong."

In trying to recover from the octopuslike grip of the disease concept of present treatment ideology, several ideas emerge. (1) Any person who drinks can develop an alcohol problem (2) recovery from the habit of alcoholic drinking can mean either abstinence or moderate drinking (3) Persons with alcohol problems are extremely diverse and have little in common except their addiction to alcohol (4) Their drinking problem is typically intertwined with a cluster of other life-problems, none of which can be separated from the environment, and (5) Social, vocational, and economic stress must also be considered causitive factors which could lead to remission in an overdrinker, just as a person with a broken leg might feel it collapse under him if sufficient pressure were brought to bear on it. In other words, let us not look only at the individual and his alcoholic response to stress, but to the system that is oppressing him for change, improvement, and true concern.

As Doctors Mark and Linda Sobell suggest: "The question asked is how many persons consistently deny that they have a drinking problem until they have truly become chronic alcoholics—and how much is such a denial based upon a resistance to being condemned to abstinence for life?

"Any effective form of therapy must consider the kinds of behaviors which our society reinforces. If the goal of therapy is to be abstinence, then the patient must be prepared to identify with abstinent social groups (Alcoholics Anonymous, certain religious groups, etc.) which specifically reinforce nondrinking. If the patient cannot or chooses not to identify with social groups supportive of abstinence, then the constraint of nondrinking might actually act as a stressor for the patient, rather than a support. the majority of our society reinforces a pattern of moderate drinking. (For ex-alcoholics, a more descriptive term would be controlled drinking.) If this is the treatment goal which is most practical and beneficial for a given individual, it should be pursued."

chapter 5

Alcoholics Anonymous:
the Pro and the Con

Back in 1935, when cofounders, Bill W. and Dr. Bob S. founded AA, even in their wildest imaginings they couldn't have foreseen the impact it would have on future generations. These two formerly "hopeless drunks," as they described themselves, left a mark on our entire civilization. Aldous Huxley called Bill W. the "greatest social architect of the century." Inspiration for the AA movement came from many sources, including the Oxford Movement, the Woman's Temperance Union, Dr. Silkworth, and the writings of William James and Dr. Carl Jung. Dr. Jung had compared the thirst for heavy drinking to infantile longings. Bill W. had belonged to the Oxford Group with roots in Christian fundamentalism, founded by a Lutheran minister. That AA has helped many is uncontested. Until recently, it had become as unquestioned in virtue as motherhood, the flag, or apple pie.

While formerly considered "on the side of the angels," AA has literally been a friend to the friendless and has been especially comforting to the Bowery poor and other skid row types. Surely it will always continue where it is most effective, in dealing with those at death's door. Like Caesar's wife, who was deemed "beyond suspicion," so, for many years, it was considered heresy in the field to question any of its tenets, which are looked at almost as divine revelation by believers, apart from and not in need of scientific validation. Yet, today, more and more critical voices are heard. Some state that it has an unequivocal stranglehold on the entire field of alcoholism treatment and prevention, or that AA influences government policy too much, or AA strongly opposes research and engages in what can only be called "benevolent despotism" and "aggressive evangelism."

AA influence and what functions as its voice on the media level, the National Council on Alcoholism is a powerful force in our society. Their concepts have become deeply entrenched and have moved into almost every area of American life: the schools, hospitals, courts, industries, the military and even into the White House! Alcohol is big business. The federal government's largest source of tax revenue, second only to that from federal income taxes, is from the vast liquor industry.

AA's ideas have become part of the alcohol establishment, which includes the federal government's role. And Uncle Sam spends money! For the central authority of the National Institute of Alcohol Abuse and Alcoholism, a funding of 600.5 million dollars has been authorized over a three year period, under the Hughes Act. Since 1975, federal funds for alcohol prevention and education alone are in excess of $75 million and the effectiveness of these programs has been called into question, since teen drinking, as well as drinking in all age groups, is on the increase.

Sales of AA's several books and pamphlets are approaching $1,500,000 annually. The third edition of the "Big Book", as it is called by Alcoholics Anonymous has recently been published. AA World Services says that at least one million four hundred and fifty thousand hardcover copies of the first and second edition have been sold since 1939, with translations into nine foreign languages. (It sells for $6.95. Box 459, Grand Central Station, New York, N.Y. 10017). In a 1976 news release, AA World Services Organization claimed a membership of more than one million with twenty-eight thousand groups meeting in ninety countries. The figures speak for themselves and, undeniably, many have found help through "the miracle of AA" and "all the love and warmth in these rooms."

Of AA successes, not much space will be given in this chapter: it needs no championing. In fact, its concepts have invaded almost every phase of current society, affecting medical, social, judicial, penal, corporate, and government policies. No stone was left unturned—and no alcoholic is to be left undetected by the new, early identification campaigns or untreated by "constructive coercion" techniques. It has become a vast monopoly in the field of alcoholism treatment (less and less, however, a program of attraction and more and more one of compulsion. Judge: "Go to AA or thirty days in jail!")

Back in the 1930s, not only was AA born, but also the behavioral approach to psychology was put into use—and these two approaches have been "uneasy bedfellows" ever since. To AA, alcoholism is a disease, an allergy of the body, plus a mental obsession. To the behaviorists, it is simply a behavior pattern in need of modification or change. While the disease model was a way of giving the alcoholic a better break in society, some say, by making him sick instead of bad and opening the door to certain benefits, it has created many problems.

In recent years, there has been a shift away from studying the psyche to simply observing how people behave. The behaviorists shy away from the medical model and also from a mental approach. They believe there is no evidence that biological causes exist for many behavioral problems. The AA folk-myth approach is, of course, not compatible with that of the behavioral scientists; nor in fact, with the ever increasing portion of the general public who has been educated in the behavioral scientists' thinking by the popular psychology books.

One critic said: "AA is a Sunday school approach to a sophisticated problem." Another former AA comented, "In the beginning, when they confined themselves to true alcoholics, real, nonfunctioning types, they were okay; but when they tried to railroad every American housewife who drinks into AA, they lost credibility!"

How does AA work? It reinforces the alcoholic's desire to stop drinking. ("The only requirement is an honest desire to stop drinking.") However, many drinkers are lost on just this one point. They really don't want to stop—at least not forever—but rather, to cut down. They want to be able to drink without getting into trouble. Such people won't find any help in AA, whose philosophy amounts to saying: "Go out and get sicker, before we'll help." As written in AA's inflexible doctrine, there are three basic prerequisites for recovery from alcoholism: (1) The alcoholic must desire to be treated, (2) he must want to stick with treatment, and (3) he must want to recover, as defined by a total lifetime of abstention from alcohol. According to AA, unless the alcoholic accepts the fact that he can *never again* touch alcohol in any form, any treatment will only be temporary.

Thus, AA is *not* a cure for alcoholism. (They do not believe one exists.) AA is a way of treating alcohol imbibers in which members themselves act as "therapists" to each other, setting up what Dr. Eric Berne called the role of the alcoholic and alcoholic game playing. What AA does *not* do, as is clearly stated, is to provide motivation for recovery, keep records or case histories, make medical or psychological diagnoses, provide drying out services, or provide any professional, medical, or psychological help whatsoever.

The true AA member is not psychologically oriented, as he believes all his needs are taken care of in AA. Thus, a possible source of life help is cut off. Only recently have psychologists and psychiatrists taken an interest in having alcoholics as patients, formerly believing them to be "orally regressed neurotics," "impossible to help," and "recidivistic." Until recently, most psychologists joined with medical men in shunting them into AA practically at the mention of a "drinking problem." So AA has become a kind of catchall for people with a variety of problems who nobody knew what to do with—and for whom a quick diagnosis of alcoholism became the easy solution.

Thus, for example, persons with a primary problem of depression, for which the overdrinking was only a symptom, could end up with a misdiagnosis of alcoholism and the prescription of a lifetime of AA meetings and no alcohol. In AA, depression is not tolerated. It's interpreted as "self-pity" rather than being recognized as a condition that can be helped through counseling, antidepression medications, anhedonia therapy, etc. Dr. Nathan Kline calls depression "our most untreated disease" and estimates 20 million Americans suffer from it, double the estimated number of 10 million given for alcoholics.

In waiting for the drinker to "hit bottom," there is no attempt made at prevention and no attention is given to help the person to moderate his habits, before arriving at late-stage alcoholism. Moreover, forceful "leverage" may be used, such as a threat of, or actual loss of, job, spouse, or children, in order to bring the alcoholic to his knees or "bottom." One mother who had never laid a hand on her children, was turned over to the Child Protective League, an arm of the law for "child abuse", because, as an AA member said: "No drinking mother can be a good mother." In some cases, dry professionals have called the police to bring in "known alcoholics," who were *not* drunk, but heard to be *drinking*, for hospitalization for alcoholism against their will, on a nonvoluntary status for compulsory treatment. This is a do-gooder stance that can only be called fascistic.

Another important criticism of AA is that too much time must be spent at AA meetings, possibly inducing the person to neglect family, friends, career ambitions, and other projects and responsibilities. If the alcoholic isn't "getting the program," the prescription is, invariably, that he/she must attend more meetings. Some AAs think nothing of attending as many as three meetings a day, and go to some meeting every day, or evening, seven days a week—for their entire lives!

The researchers Gerard, Wile and Saenger, in an evaluation of AA "successes," suggested that total abstinence, for some, could only be achieved at the expense of effective functioning in other areas of life. "The abstinent AA may not drink but it may cost him a total investment of time, interest, and energy . . . and the absorption with AA for some becomes an obsessional or fetishistic devotion." The researchers noted that patients in their sample with continued AA dependence, had "constricted social, vocational and psychological dysfunction," due to what others have called the "dysfunctional aspects" of AA. As Dr. E. Mansell Pattison has suggested in his paper: "A Critique of Alcoholism Treatment Concepts," the maintenance of abstinence is possible only at a high price in terms of time and psychic energy. The true AA member becomes as addicted to AA meetings as he formerly was to alcohol. And this must continue for the rest of his life or he will endanger his sobriety, thought to be the most important thing in his life. One former AA member commented; "To see grown men celebrating the yearly anniversary of staying away from one drink with cakes, candles, and ice cream is just too ridiculous! You'd think it was an event comparable to writing a Beethoven symphony, discovering penicillin, or climbing Mt. Everest. I was at one such 'birthday party' that was so lavish, a professional baritone was called in to sing 'Happy Birthday' to a huge crowd, who wildly applauded. I'm sure men arriving back from Antarctica never received such a reception!"

Thus, the AA alcoholic is never to be weaned from his dependency on AA, his "crutch." Self-sufficiency, autonomy, self-reliance, and independence are not encouraged. At every meeting he has to say: "I am an alcoholic." He comes to think of himself as a "sickee." He doesn't function well alone and must have the support of the group. Moreover, it is believed he can only keep his sobriety by helping the "still-suffering alcoholic". While billed as a program of attraction, members are actually encouraged to go out and get new members, multiplying the strength of the membership, as a way of saving themselves. This leads to manipulative social engineering in order to get new disciples or converts.

"Slips" from abstention in AA are not tolerated, ("Stick with the winners, Honey.") And it is clearly stated in AA literature: "The moment he willingly drinks so much as a drop of beer, wine, spirits, or any other alcoholic drink, he automatically loses all status in AA. AA is not interested in sobering up drunks who are not sincere in sobering up for all time."

Yet, even if AA were able to help all alcoholics, and statistics say it is only reaching 5 percent of these, we are told only one out of every eleven drinkers is an alcoholic. What about the other ten?

Are they not entitled to some help? AA members, preferring to wait for alcoholics to hit bottom, which usually involves hospitalization, loss of job, home, spouse, or legal complications, such as a DWI (Driving-While-Intoxicated) summons, law suits, etc., offer no help here. And the blunt truth is, despite the millions of dollars being spent for funding official programs, most alcoholics who leave treatment drink again—and again!

In a trend of increasing criticism of AA, its critics have come up with some points worth considering. One complaint is that in AA there is an appalling indifference to good nutrition, vitamins, and health regiments. AA emphasizes cakes, sweets, coffee, and soft drinks to such an extent that famous nutritionist Adele Davis commented: "It's a wonder AAs can stay sober at all, considering all the coffee and cake consumed." Poor nutrition, some believe, sets up a blood sugar imbalance that could be responsible for the 'alcoholic craving' for drink.

Another important point is that alcohol, in AA, is still the most important thing in the person's life, with the emphasis switched from drinking to *not* drinking. Instead of moving the alcoholic spirits from *central* focus to the periphery of the lifestyle, AAs spend an awful lot of time talking about alcohol and drinking, *ad nauseum*. AA members substitute talking about drinking for the act of drinking, leading to an overemphasis on verbalization (as if it was interchangeable in satisfaction with direct action).

Another frequent criticism of AA is that *all* the alcoholic's life problems are seen as a *result* of his drinking. The demon "King Alcohol" is scapegoated and convicted of causing the life to become "unmanageable" even when the person had serious troubles many years before he ever picked up that first drink. This is explained away as a result of his "alcoholic personality" and "dry drunks."

Yet, life really has its inequities, to which some are admittedly more sensitive than others, and a power structure that places many at a disadvantage. We learn in physics that different metals have different breaking points directly related to heat or stress. Are people any different?

The alcoholic is told: "You drink because you *are* an alcoholic" when, in fact, some situational drinkers only drink alcoholically when subjected to extreme stress. These drinkers should look for the reasons *why* they overdrink. They should not be encouraged to switch symptoms, to change the overdrinking symptom and become a hypochondriac, a pill popper, a workaholic, a candyholic, a religious fanatic, or to be purposively accident-prone or sexually promiscuous.

The alcohol establishment has also been accused of excessive use of scare tactics. For example, any lapse of memory or absent-mindedness is interpreted as "irreversible, brain damage" and the overdrinker is taunted with the possible spectre of DTs (delirium tremens) which is equated with almost certain death. Yet medical statistics show that delirium tremens, when severe, have a fatality rate of only about 8%—not 100%! The threat of liver damage is forcefully brought home to the alcoholic. While it's true that cirrhosis of the liver occurs in about 8% of alcoholics, as compared to 1% in nonalcoholics, that is still a rather small percentage. While it's true that the percentage of suicides that involve alcoholics is 31%, it is equally true that 69% do not. The AA alcoholic is taught to fear reaching one of two unpleasant conditions before demise: either "wet brain" or "alcoholic insanity." This is not to say that these conditions do not exist, but rather that it's an exaggeration to say that *every* alcoholic who resumes drinking is assured of going the madness route or becoming a total vegetable.

Pictures of carnage on the highways are also shown at some AA-type facilities. At the same time, the alcoholic is told if he picks up *one* drink, *anything* may happen, and probably will. He is told he can't control his alcohol intake because of his "obsession." The power of suggestion alone could be enough to cause accidents, especially when combined with the implicit idea given alcoholics that they are irresponsible, impulsive people who lack reliability and loving concern for others as well as a sense of community responsibility.

If we fashion a well-defined role in our society called "alcoholic," we can well expect some of those we cast into it to act it out to the hilt! (This prompted one former AA to say: "If you're not an alcoholic when you go into AA, you soon will be." Another ex-AA member claimed: "I had to drop out of AA, before I *became* an alcoholic!"

Surprisingly, in speaking of car accidents, a recent study showed that it is the social drinker, rather than the chronic alcoholic who is the most likely to have a car accident. He is over-confident of his ability to handle alcohol and does not clearly know his own capacity. Many confirmed alcoholics, fearing accidents above all, don't drive or make it a point never to drive while drinking.

One researcher feels that the strict, prohibitionistic attitude of AA towards alcohol makes a person feel extremely guilty for any slip, although this slip could have been harmless social drinking.

The AA disease concept makes alcoholism a progressive, terminal disease and this is strongly impressed on all members. But also, for the 'losers' slips tend to become progressively wilder and more dangerous. These slips usually end on a tragic note: jail, hospitalization, accident, homicide, or suicide attempt. He observed that chronic overdrinkers, not in AA, tended to be more stabilized in their drinking, less on a downward collision course of self-destructiveness. He said, in fact, "that the drinking ability of these people may improve with time, in regard to less quantity consumed and fewer troublesome aftereffects." He felt that the "guilt-load" of AA made the crucial difference.

One AA dropout called AA a "baffling and insidious" program, which are just the words AAs' use to describe alcoholism. She found AA to be anti-joy, puritanical, and punitive, the latter being evidenced by the necessity of having to "make amends," under threat that he or she will lose his sobriety. Another common objection to AA is the "public confessional" approach. It is thought that the endless listening to "drunkalogues" can result in the listener making a negative identification with the speaker, instead of a positive one. One AA dropout said: "They teach you how to be an alcoholic, if you don't already know!" If the overdrinker romantically identifies with the wild escapades, especially when most of the story concerns this, rather than how to stop or correct drinking procedures, he may want to glamorize his own story by actually doing and then telling about the "awful things I did on my last slip." Yet, one AA member, who is in and out of the program, said: "Listening to those far-out tales of 'How I Went to Hell and Back' is far the most fun-filled and fascinating part of AA. Otherwise, it would be incredibly *boring!*"

Another AA dropout exclaimed that "the meetings are much too dull and creepy. The cure has become *worse* than the disease!" In listening to all these stories, one notes a degree of gamesmanship in the "competitive suffering." If you hear the same life story told by the same person over a period of years, you are struck by the fact the stories often change dramatically. They tend to grow more alike, as if they had come to be written by the collective AA group-mind. Former AA people have confessed that they found themselves grossly exaggerating, if not telling downright lies, in order to make the drinking the cause of all their problems! Done repeatedly, this tendency to falsify reality can become a bad habit. One AA member said: "I quit the day I heard myself tell how I was experiencing a religious awakening in the middle of an AA meeting. It was just too embarrassing." Another said: "I had to quit the day I heard myself say things I don't believe at all."

A psychiatrist notes that the program fosters passivity and fatality, rather than self-assertion and creative maturity. Self-sacrifice, meekness, humility, compliance, and conformity to group ideals are stressed. This reinforces underachieving, complacency, resignation, and a weak ego structure. Constructive rebellion is totally discouraged. (The race horse is to be content behind the plow.) Since the most important thing is to "stay away from one drink, one day at a time," the importance of work, achievement, conquest, human relations, making money, fighting for a cause, or standing up for one's rights is undervalued. Economic illiteracy is encouraged. (The poor alcoholic is to stay *poor!*) Not drinking, in itself, becomes synonymous with virtue, rather than the idea that it doesn't matter if you drink or don't drink—as long as you don't harm yourself or others.

There is too much negative brainwashing in the form of statements such as : "If you pick up one drink, you won't be able to stop and terrible things will happen." Persons are not permitted to try to gain control over their alcohol habit and learn to drink non-abusively, if so desired. Then, too, AA necessitates a complete change of lifestyle for most people, who are advised to give up their old drinking companions, even if these people happen to include the employer or business contacts that are vital. (The drinker will be advised to seek other employment, even at a large salary cut.) In the end, the AA-oriented life places and confines the drinker to a secluded AA "hothouse environment," rather than mainstreaming him back into a normal social environment where there is both drinking and abstention.

Much criticism has been leveled at the religious aspect of AA with its implicit idea that if you are drinking you cannot be leading a religious life. (Nondrinking becomes equated with sainthood.) Members are told to take a "searching and fearless moral inventory" and to "admit to God, ourselves, and another human being the exact nature of our wrongs." But not everyone who has a drinking problem is interested in a complete character change, especially older people. Others are simply unable to achieve the complete "spiritual transformation" which AA members believe is essential for permanent recovery from alcoholism. Nor do they desire to confess all before another human being: "naked and stripped of all pretence."

In keeping with the "you're okay, I'm okay" philosophy of modern psychology, they believe that they are already highly principled, generally law-abiding citizens, ethical, moral people, not lacking in spiritual insight. But the missionary zeal of recovered AA members assumes that all persons who have a drinking problem are in some stage of alcoholismic deterioration. Yet, not many overdrinkers are willing to admit to being self-indulgent hedonists or semibarbaric pagans in need of religious conversion. They are also not willing to assert that "no human power could relieve our alcoholism" or that they are "powerless over alcohol." These people feel that when you say you cannot "manage your life," it is tantamount to issuing an invitation to others to step in and take control, which too often leads to the condition of "too many cooks spoil the broth." Nor do they incline to a creed of unnecessary self-sacrifice, though according to "Twelve Steps and Twelve Traditions": "The spiritual substance of anonymity *is* sacrifice." (You, as you, do not exist, except as a vehicle of "good works.") Some drinkers do *not* aspire to a halo of complete saintliness, or martyrdom, but simply need some help with a drinking problem. (To this, AA members would bring the charge of *'Stinkin' thinkin',* reserved for any anti-AA comments.) In the ultimate pursuit of serenity, there often comes a desire to be confronted with no unpleasantness whatsoever. The fighting spirit is squelched. This can lead to "milktoastism", a "peace at any price," which often has a terrible price. Lack of assertiveness leads to diminishment of personal ambitions for achievement or any social or economic upward mobility. It creates a complete *dis*-inclination for competition and free enterprise. ("The pursuit of money, personal power, prestige and public honors are disastrous to us.") The AA alcoholic is to be satisfied with humble pie, and a very small piece of the pie at that. And he is not to have his *own will* at his *own disposal*, but to turn it over to his Higher Power or that of the group.

A psychiatrist says that the disease model encourages immaturity in that, as a patient, the alcoholic may expect to be taken care of or granted special privileges. He need not assume as much responsibility for himself as he is 'sick' and, as such, demands our attention, concern, and consideration. AA has also been criticized for its arbitrary way of diagnosing alcoholism: "You are one if you say you are, and only *you* can make the final judgement." It is certainly the only self-diagnosing disease and the only one where the patient is not permitted to evidence his symptom.

Booze, *per se*, is considered a poison, rather than a neutral spirit that can become good or bad, according to how you use it. As an AA member you are told: "You are only *one* drink away from a drunk in which you may lose everything." The alcoholic is told quite devastatingly that he is "sick mentally, spiritually, and physically." (This doesn't leave him much to work with!) AA members are treated as one of a group-type, rather than any emphasis being placed on biochemical individuality or uniqueness. Mindless conformity is looked upon as a sign of mental health, when it could signify the opposite: stagnation, wasted potentialities, and abandoned talents, the giving up of a dream.

AA members are made to feel guilty for having feelings of anger, even though justified, rather than being taught sensible ways of coping with hostility, fear, and aggression. Alcoholics are often accused of being 'paranoid' when, in truth, they may not be suspicious enough before the fact. Someone may indeed be trying to take advantage of them being as they are so often introverted, gentle people, not skilled in self-protective techniques.

Finally, once the overdrinker accepts the label "alcoholic," he is stigmatized for life. And there *is* an interchange of information between the mental health centers, the hospitals, the schools, potential employers, insurance companies, motor vehicle depts., etc. This label can adversely affect the overdrinker in every area of his life: socially, psychologically, economically, vocationally and politically. (And what is most maddening is that AA members when confronted with an ex-member successfully doing controlled drinking will say "he never was an alcoholic!")

The truth is many overdrinkers are turned off by AA. Only 5% of the total 10 million estimated US alcoholics are AA members and of these every year some drop out. It has been suggested that even some of those in AA don't actually belong there, never having had the problem. Some of these include a counselor looking for patients, a salesman wanting more business, a young lawyer eager to pick up DWI cases (now at $750 each), and lonely hearts, seeking a social or sex life, and who are disgusted with the bar scene.

AA has been criticized for being a closed system and not seeking improvement or change. (No updating in forty years.) Intelligence is considered a drawback. One sponsor said: "The less intelligent the person, the easier time he'll have in picking up the program. When I see somebody well-read and asking a lot of questions, I know this person is going to have a hard time making it in AA."

AA has no interest in research of any sort. They are admittedly hostile to "cures" such as those reported by advocates of megavitamin therapy. While AA adopted the medical model of alcoholism (some say invented it), no medication is ever given and no medical help offered in any AA facilities. As John Cashman observed: "It's the only disease where doctors refer you to faith healers . . ."

Mr. Cashman wrote in his article, "And Never a Drop to Drink" (*Newsday*, June 23, 1976): "AA has created many of the problems it refuses to help solve. It was AA's early and over-publicized successes that gave the disease concept, the incurability of alcoholism and the need for total abstinence their respectability . . .

"None of this is meant to belittle the work of AA. It is simply that much of the dogmatic righteousness and folk medicine that now bedevils the field of alcoholism has been produced by AA. Whatever quarrel there is would not be with AA but with its commanding position in the mainstream of alcoholism treatment and theory.

"In much the same way, nobody would argue with the right of Christian Scientists to dictate beliefs to their members. But, if Christian Science began to dictate public health policy, there would be grounds for opposition, not to Christian science itself, but to its impact on all non-Christian Scientists."

Why is it necessary to evaluate AA? Why can't we sneak other programs in the back door, so to speak, compromise a bit here and there, and not step on AA's toes? Because if AA were doing the job for the majority of alcoholics, there would be no vital need for other programs. And had it fulfilled the great promise of its early years, alcoholism would not be reaching near epidemic proportions today. There are just *too many* losers, too many drop-outs . . . too many suicides. From this, we must deduce that they're doing something wrong, *albeit* from the noblest of motives. Also an appraisal of AA strengths and weaknesses can be of inestimable value in structuring new programs. Surely all future programs will be beholden to AA and acknowledge a debt to it, but not be restricted by it. In the field of scientific research, nothing and no one should be above criticism. Clear-cut data, rather than cherished dogma, must prevail.

Of course, there will *always* be an AA—and rightly so. But I believe it has reached its peak of dominance and in the next ten years there will be room for other modalities. Many new and exciting programs now springing up will take root, offering the alcohol-abuser a number of options for treatment. In moments of nostalgia for "the old ways," many of us will lament the waning of its powers, with the sadness one always feels for the dying of a beloved father. But the future will not be stopped. And to those with eyes to see and ears to hear, all signs now point in new directions.

chapter 6

Treatment Centers:

the Old and the New

Not so long ago drunkenness was considered evil by the church; deviant behavior by the civil authorities; and criminal behavior by the police. And until recently alcoholics were thought to be difficult to treat and incurable. Doctors would refuse to accept them as patients. If they could be motivated to change or could be frightened into abstinence, they would be sent to AA. (If they continued their "nasty habit," it was predicted they would end up in a general hospital, jail, or morgue.) There was no other treatment for them. Today there are an estimated ten thousand treatment facilities, mostly offering the traditional regimen, but some now offering new and exciting programs.

Most of the centers offer no medical treatment but a fourteen-day involuntary or voluntary hospital stay, which consists mainly of detoxification and compulsory attendance at AA meetings with possibly some medication. Welfare recipients can have this paid for by Medicaid or Medicare. It is not cheap, running around $120-$150 a day. The common element in most of the cures is group support ("treating people with people") and because of the unavailability of alcohol, it offers the alcoholic a chance to defuzz his mind from alcoholic thinking and to sober up.

Typical of the traditional treatment programs is Chit Chat Farms in Reading, Pa. Jim Byran is director of therapy. He says: "We tell the patients it can be done, and you don't have to do it alone. The patients help each other get well." The staff, including Jim Byran, are typically recovered alcoholics. (A twenty-eight-day stay at Chit Chat runs a minimum of $840.) Bryan says, "We don't look into the *whys* of drinking but only *how* you can stop."

Treatment at Lutheran General Hospital, in Chicago, Ill., runs $1,827 for a twenty-one-day stay. Here, also, there is an emphasis on interaction between staff and patients and patients and other patients, helping to cure each other. Patients at Lutheran General are treated for any withdrawal symptoms and given a medical assessment. In group sessions, patients meet three times a week, in many cases with family members; sometimes even employers are included.

At Seattle's Shick's Shadel Hospital, group therapy is combined with hypnotic suggestion and aversion treatment, consisting of electric shocks or drugs to make the very odor of liquor abhorrent. This treatment runs eleven days at a cost of approximately fifteen hundred dollars. In the hospital's simulated bar, which is called "Duffy's Tavern," the patient is given a nausea inducing shot and then handed a glass of his favorite drink. He sniffs it, sips it, and then—sickened—he throws up.

The patient goes through this process four more times. At the end of treatment, presumably, he will associate nausea with liquor and have developed, hopefully, a longtime aversion to alcohol in any form. The hospital's director, Dr. James W. Smith, says: "Aversion therapy is not fun at all . . . but you are dealing with a fatal illness . . . In other fatal illnesses, such as cancer, surgery is often called for if it gives the patient the best fighting chance for survival. At the moment, this is the best we know of—the method that will do the best job in the shortest time." It is interesting to note that in response to criticism of European punishment for drunkenness (traditionally, forty lashes) Dr. Malik Badri, of Saudi Arabia, replied that he feels that "in comparison to some methods of Western aversion therapy, using drugs to induce repeated vomiting, or electroshock, for example, flogging cannot be considered cruel."

Aversion therapy then, indeed, has been highly criticized by some experts. A program that draws even more controversy is the "wet" experimental one at Coatesville Veterans Administration Hospital in Pennsylvania, directed by Dr. Edward Gottheil. He claims that traditional programs either study alcoholics without alcohol or alcohol without alcoholics, but not the drinking itself. He says further, "The idea that abstinence is the only treatment. . .interferes with research."

At Coatesville, patients are given individual psychotherapy, group therapy, music therapy and antidrinking seminars. They are also permitted to drink once an hour on-the-hour between 9:00 A.M. and 9:00 P.M., if they ask for it. So that thirteen times a day, the patient must make a decision to drink or not to drink. In the follow up study of the first group, they claim that after six months half the group members were either dry or drinking less than twice a week.

Only a few alcoholics in the US receive the variety of help

available at the Mendocino California's State Hospital Center for Alcoholism and Drug Abuse. The patients here can choose his or her own method of treatment from among such methods as automatic relaxation, guided daydreaming, gut level confrontation, nonverbal communications, behavior modification through reinforcement techniques, and group therapy.

The Walk-in Counseling Center, founded in 1969 in Minneapolis, is designed to provide immediate help for people who will not or cannot find it elsewhere. No appointments are necessary. There are no eligibility requirements, no fees, no hassle. Focus is on the client's definition of the problem, not the counselor's, and alternatives to dealing with it. Besides individuals and couples, families are also welcome. Alcohol and drug problems are evaluated and treated. (For information write The Walk-In Counseling Center, 2421 Chicago Ave., S. Minneapolis, Minn. 55404.)

La Hacienda, in Hunt, Texas, is one of the most luxurious of the drying out places. During the guest's day, which runs from 8:00 A.M. to 9:00 P.M., every day except Sunday, he may be involved in individual, group, or family counseling: videotape training; relaxation and stress reduction therapy; informational seminars, utilizing speakers, films, and tapes; and area field trips.

Situated on approximately thirty-seven acres, the buildings reflect their past history as a resort hotel. Recreational facilities include swimming pool, sauna, game and hobby rooms, hiking and fishing facilities, tennis courts, golf courses, and a bowling alley. Private accommodations are available to encourage the guest's spouse to join in the therapeutic program in the lovely setting in the Texas hills, seventy-five miles north of San Antonio.

One of their recovered alcoholics had this to say about her stay there: "La Hacienda not juta place in the hills ... It is an experience in knowing and sharing, a chance to change, to begin again, to give and receive love, to renew life ... I developed friendships with some of these people that will carry on and sustain me for a long time ... Mainly, I guess, because they helped me discover what love really is. Whatever I thought it was before, I learned that love means reaching out to another person to tell him how things *really* are with you, in your deepest heart, and hoping that he tells you back something of himself ..."

At Patton State Hospital, San Bernardino, Calif., patients begin their five week journey to sobriety by getting smashed! With the companionship of normal drinkers they are allowed to order as many as sixteen one ounce drinks. Then the party's over and they are presented with a nonelectric shock: a videotaped presentation of their drunken behavior! Most are embarrassed and dismayed by the revelations. They observe themselves gulping drinks straight, long after the normal drinkers have quit. This is part of training to be sober.

Patton State Hospital, San Bernardino, Calif., is one of the few in the country that offers a choice of therapeutic goals: either abstinence or controlled drinking. In the cocktail lounge, installed in the hospital, which boasts a polished mahogany bar, soft lights, and music, there are free drinks, a TV camera, and electronic equipment under the bar, which can administer shocks to the patients as the bartender-therapist wills. The therapeutic drinking program was suggested by psychologists Halmuth Schaefer and Dr. Mark Sobell, who disagree with the traditional view that alcoholism is based on a physiological craving. They believe it is a psychological ailment, a learned response to stress, which can be unlearned. Electric shocks are given, for example, to drinkers who drink too fast, from an electrode that has been attached to the patient's hand, or you might say *student's* hand, as this is an educational process rather than a cure.

Those who aspire to be social drinkers may drink as many as three mixed drinks before getting a shock. Those on an abstinence program will not be allowed any. The social drinker must make each drink last 20 minutes. Six months later, from 50% to 70% so trained were either abstinent or successfully moderating.

Dr. Ovide Pomerleau is director of the University of Pennsylvania's Center for Behavioral Medicine at Philadelphia, Pa., which specializes in helping people develop more self-control, especially in regard to overdrinking and oversmoking. He says, "Like any other behavior, overdrinking is subject to the environment. Any amount of alcohol, no matter how small, does not trigger the same response in the body. It's not as if the excessive drinker is a heroin addict in need of a fix. After a two week bout, an alcoholic who stops drinking will have withdrawal symptoms. But when he dries out, he's no longer addicted. He has a *habituation*. So he has to dismantle the habits which make up the pattern."

Dr. Pomerleau is enthusiastic about the use of behavior modification techniques. He says: "They may prove as important in improving health and increasing longevity as was the development of effective, antibacterial agents in the first half of the century." His therapists use behavior modification techniques to help clients (he does not call them patients) to deal with problems of self-control (oversmoking, overdrinking, or overeating).

The whole process of treating alcoholics in the past, he says, was "almost religious." "As a sinner, the alcoholic was asked to repent. As part of his penance, he had to state verbally that he would never indulge again," says Pommerleau. "At the same time, patients were permitted to view their alcoholism as a disease over which they had no control. And so they didn't have to take responsibility for what happened during their drunk bouts." But Dr. Pommerleau doesn't view alcoholism as a disease. He tells drinkers they are responsible for their own lives and must control their habits "with a little help from your friends here at the center.

"We do not push abstinence; because if we have inflexible goals that we try to push on everyone, a lot of people who need help probably aren't going to get it. If we make our program more flexible, we feel it is more attractive. Our concern is with reaching people who have *not* hit bottom . . ." Dr. John Paul Brady, chairman of Penn's psychiatry department, says: "Anyone who is able to adopt the attitude that he wants to be a master of his own fate, to a greater degree than now, and who recognizes that he can have more self-control—but who needs a coach, can benefit here."

In a study, a comparison of behavioral and traditional treatment for middle income problem drinkers, conducted at the University of Pa., department of psychiatry, 72% of behavioral participants were improved at the year's anniversary point with only 11% dropping out, compared with 50% of traditional participants improved, with 43% dropping out. When "abstinent days" and "controlled-drinking days" were combined under the heading "functioning well," the percentage of clients "functioning well" 80% or more of the time was as follows: 79% "functioning well" in the behavior modification group, versus 22% in the traditional control group. Therapy is conducted in ninety-minute sessions meeting once a week for three months. (There is a pretreatment fee required, on a sliding scale, from $85 to $500, based on ability to pay.)

Dr. Roger F. Vogler's Alcohol Abuse Program in Pomona, California, is aimed at the early stage alcohol abuser who has the personal and financial resources to do something about his problem at a time when it is most amenable to change. Clients are offered a choice of therapeutic goals: either abstinence or controlled drinking. Dr. Vogler, who got his doctorate in psychology from the University of Arizona at Tuscon in 1967, is an associate professor of psychology at Pomona College and at Claremont Graduate School. Ten years of experimental research have gone into the development of his programs.

All clients are first assessed to determine the probability of suc-

cess in a moderation treatment program. The basis for this evaluation is derived from research. If the client has a high probablity of
succeeding in moderation and the person accepts the financial
obligation involved, he/she will be accepted into the program. The
client is charged an hourly rate of $45.00 for each hour of training
received. This usually amounts to a total fee of between five
hundred and one thousand dollars, depending on progress.

Most of the sessions are for two hours each and involve the consumption of alcohol in a simulated bar equipped with closed cir-
cuit television and breath analysis devices. Weekly sessions are
held for about two months, after which hourly sessions are held at
bimonthly intervals. The total time in training is usually about two
months, with occasional booster sessions over the next year to assure durability of effects.

Dr. Vogler dislikes the term alcoholic and uses it sparingly, preferring "alcohol abuser." He firmly believes that some—not all—
alcohol abusers can learn to become moderate drinkers. He also
believes there are some people who should never pick up a drink.
"If a person drinks more than a fifth of liquor a day, has been doing it for fifteen or twenty years, has lost a lot of jobs because of
drinking, comes from a less-than-stable marital relationship, he's a
poor risk and we wouldn't take him." He will, however, take a
person who drinks a bit less, is vocationally stable, but may have
gotten into some trouble with the law, and who, perhaps, has an intact marriage and no physical damage.

The essential training component of his program is videotaped, self-confrontation of intoxicated behavior to elicit the
motivation to change and to rapidly derive information about the
function of alcohol in the drinker's life. There is also training to
estimate the blood alcohol level under various conditions; alcohol
education, oriented toward the practical aspects of using alcohol;
and alternatives training to establish competing activities for excessive drinking. And he gives behavioral counseling to deal with personal problems related to the consumption of alcohol.

The usual reaction to seeing drunk behavior videotaped, is that
the overdrinker is ashamed and embarrassed—and determined to
drink in a controlled fashion in the future—or not at all. It doesn't
work with everyone, however, he says, as a few people think it's
funny. Once you get a person motivated to change, then, as Dr.
Vogler says: "What we do is be very nosy about his daily schedule,
find out those times and those persons he associates with drinking,
then attempt to establish some alternative activities that would not

involve drinking."

The Blood Alcohol Discrimination training helps the abuser to estimate his exact degree of intoxication. "We help a person identify what thirty milligrams percent blood alcohol is and what fifty milligrams percent is, so he can say, 'I should stop here.' " Dr. Vogler regards anything over fifty milligrams percent blood alcohol as immoderate drinking. (In California, one hundred milligrams percent is legal intoxication.) "Fifty is too damn drunk to drive a car," says Vogler. His program also involves showing abusers how to resist social pressure to drink: how to say "no" to a drink.

Those in the Pomona program, in one study, showed that all subjects made significant changes in such things as intake reduction. Vogler said: "A year after training, a third were moderate drinkers, another third were abstinent, and another third relapsed. Now the fact that a third were moderate drinkers for a whole year after training is pretty powerful evidence that some chronic alcoholics can learn to moderate." An important point is that those chronic drinkers who got the maximum amount of training on the average changed their intake from about fifteen to three drinks per day.

The Social Learning Center, San Francisco, Calif., is run by Dr. Ronald Greene and Ms. Mary Kelley. They offer special help for the problem drinker and his or her family. They particularly want to help those who do not want to be stigmatized "alcoholic." The Social Learning Center, located at 1312-20th Ave., S.F., Calif. 94122, has an alcohol program helpful to those seeking abstinence or those who do not wish to face a lifetime of abstinence. There are few places in the Bay Area where such people can go for help, for most of the local programs adhere to the disease concept. They avoid labeling. Problem drinking is approached as a learned behavior that is maintained by the person's perception of the immediate environment, the person's own thoughts about the consequences of his or her drinking.

People in their program are taught to understand and to bring under control the environmental situations that have been green lights for excessive drinking. They are also taught how their own unrealistic thoughts bring on and maintain their negative drinking behavior, and how these self-defeating thoughts can be effectively changed. They assert that if a person believes he has no control over his drinking, after one or more drinks, he is likely to lose control. People come to the center to learn to take responsibility for all their drinking behavior, both moderate and excessive, without crippling self-blame and self-condemnation for failures.

Although they concede there may be a biological predisposition to problem drinking, the center's directors feel that these considerations are overshadowed by cultural learning. They agree, people would probably be better off leading entirely drug-free lives; but for the most of us today, this goal seems utopian. The evidence is overwhelming, the vast majority of people who drink too much continue to drink in one form or another for the rest of their lives.

Recognizing this reality, the Social Learning Center's Alcohol Program offers a choice of therapeutic goals. Procedures and techniques of the program include detailed analysis of situations that stimulate excessive drinking, cognitive restructuring, effective methods of coping with stress, problem-solving techniques, training in self-assertion, communication and interpersonal skills, sexual problem-solving, constructive ways of filling "free," non-drinking time, and aversion therapy, for those choosing abstinence and controlled drinking techniques. Fees are $35.00 per individual, and $10.00 per group session, adjusted to income. Co-director Mary Kelley is a registered nurse. The Social Learning Center also offers assertive behavior training with video feedback. Workshop members are presented with an assertive philosophy and are encouraged to challenge common misconceptions which help maintain self-defeating behavior. Each patient is given homework to practice, emphasizing assertive skills in real life situations.

The Maytag-Hoghston Clinic, 1666 Elmire, Suite 105, Aurora, Colorado has a slogan: "Fear will make people do great things—Love allows them to do the impossible." it is the intent of this fine program to provide awareness of the problems created by substance abuse, especially alcohol. Their program emphasizes self-awareness, self-integration, and self-fulfillment. They believe that adjusting to stress is not enough; changing one's behavioral makeup is in order. They assert that every person is capable of change and that substance abuse problems are not irreversible.

In addition to psychological testing, couples therapy, family therapy, reality therapy, education groups, transactional analysis groups, feelings and assertiveness groups, gestalt therapy, woman's groups, and Alcoholics Anonymous are available. (They are also currently beginning a Drinkwatcher's group under supervision of Jan Maytag.)

Fees run from $12.50 for one hour of individual therapy to $50.00 for a one and a half hour psychological evaluation, done by the well-known clinical psychologist, Dr. Chad Duane Emrick. The couples group is for two people in a relationship, whether it be marriage or merely dating. They have found over the years that alcohol is the only focal point in the relationship, even though often hearing the statement, "If only my—husband, wife or mate—would stop drinking, everything would be okay." They have found that this is not the case; many unresolved problems still will exist. Once the problem drinker is sober, these unresolved problems appear on the surface, and unless they are dealt with, the problem drinker usually resorts to his usual escape route of alcohol.

In another group, feelings and assertiveness are discussed. Clients are told: "It is okay to express any feelings and thoughts to this group. It is okay to feel good." In this group, they explore the nature of feelings, covering such areas as anger, sadness, guilt, depression, fear, helplessness, and other inadequacies felt by human beings. They say the more you get in touch with your true feelings, the more you will learn what you want and need. You will learn how to get these things through intelligent assertiveness.

In the group on transactional analysis, you are asked the important question: "Are you okay?" The therapists say it is probably the most important question you will ever have to answer. Because—whether you are aware of it or not—all the relationships with the most important people in your life are strongly influenced by a combination of how you feel about yourself (okay or not okay) and how you feel about others (okay or not okay). They discuss the "transactions" between you and other people. The therapists deal with the "games people play."

In their reality-therapy groups, there are "three Rs": (1) Responsibility (I am responsible for my behavior), (2) Right vs. Wrong (I must maintain a satisfactory standard of behavior), and (3) Reality. (I will not deny the reality of the world around me.)

A very popular program there also is Gestalt Therapy. Gestalt is a German word for which there is no exact English equivalent; it means, roughly the forming of an organized, meaningful whole. The aim of this therapy is to help you become whole, to help you become aware of, admit to, reclaim, and integrate your fragmented parts. Integration helps a person make the transition from dependency to self-sufficiency; from authoritarian outer-support to authentic inner-support. Concretely, having inner-support means that a person is able "to stand on his own two feet."

In Gestalt therapy, they look at what you are doing now. Being in the now requires dealing with unfinished business and resolving conflicts. If, for example, you have had a problem in accepting the death of a loved one, then this group would be appropriate for you.

They want you to be aware of how you feel. Can you love and accept others? In order to love and accept others, you must first feel love and acceptance for you. Here is a Gestalt Prayer, used by the group, which was written by Fritz Perls:

> *I do my thing, and you do your thing.*
> *I am not in the world to live up to your expectations,*
> *And you are not in this world to live up to mine;*
> *You are you, and I am I,*
> *And if by chance we find each other, it is beautiful,*
> *If not, it cannot be helped.*

James V. McConnell, Professor of Psychology at the University of Michigan, in talking about his Substance Abuse Program says: "Because we don't impose goals or values on our clients, because we offer affection, because we never punish or criticize, because we build on strengths instead of concentrating on weakness, because we teach control: the students have a success rate of 90% . . . We have worked with more than two thousand clients in the area in the past five years . . . all without government funds, brainwashing, or punishment."

Rational Emotive Therapy (RET) is being used successfully in alcoholism treatment. The emphasis is on developing "healthy self-interest" and eliminating self-defeating thoughts, attitudes and behavior. It is based on the writings of Dr. Albert Ellis, founder of the Institute for Advanced Study in Rational Psychotherapy in New York City. He says, "Man can live the most self-fulfilling, creative, and emotionally satisfying life by intelligently organizing his thinking."

He believes most sustained negative emotions such as depression, anxiety,anger, and guilt are almost always unnecessary and can be largely eradicated if people learn to think straight and follow this up with effective actions. Changing perceptions about oneself and one's environment is the first step in RET work and similar approaches such as, reality-therapy and Adlerian psychology. In other words, it is not people or events that are upsetting you or me. But, rather, it is our telling ourselves that these things are upsetting that makes us upset.

A generally accepted character trait of alcoholic persons is poor self-esteem. in the RET approach, the alcoholic person is not to rate himself by his action. he or she is worthwhile simply because he or she exists. By increasing self-acceptance, and by reducing feelings of anxiety about the expectations of others, some alcoholic persons have been able to learn to control their drinking. Dr. Brenda Baker, at the Problems of Daily Living Clinic at Sinai Hospital in Detroit, says that RET is particularly effective for persons who have tried and rejected other approaches or who don't wish to identify themselves as "alcoholic."

She says: "People in the early stage . . . who are looking for a solution which provides a greater emphasis on personal control are most likely to be attracted to the RET approach." Dr. Baker encourages changes in behavior, rather than gaining insight into the underlying reasons for drinking and she encourages clients to set their own goals. Many of the clients choose to control their drinking and work toward that objective by analyzing what cues precipitate their drinking. Then by either mapping a plan to avoid such situations or developing alternative behaviors, they see if these high-risk situations cannot be avoided.

Dr. Albert Grau uses RET at the Mount Manor Rehabilitation Center, Emmitsburg, Md. He says: "We believe it is irrational thinking that leads to irrational drinking." He asserts that the problem drinker has established a link between what he perceives as stress and the necessity of drinking: "You can even think of it," he says, "as a mathematical formula: stress + alcohol = relief. After a while, every time a stress situation comes up, it acts as a cue for the drinking and the alcoholic person drinks." His twenty-eight-day rehabilitation program includes RET, mandatory attendance at AA meetings, and educational and recreational activities.

Edward Garcia, associate director of training at the Institute for Advanced Study in Rational Psychotherapy in New York, claims that the RET approach is especially good with alcoholic persons who are unable or do not wish to give up drinking. "Alcoholic people," he says, "often believe they are unable to tolerate emotional pain and would rather face the familiar discomfort of their addiction than an unknown—and possibly more painful—alternative. Their behavior can be viewed as self-protective rather than self-destructive."

RET focuses on the client's irrational beliefs about his needs for approval, love, success, and comfort. In the RET view, if you change your thinking, you change your feelings. In RET, the person talks to himself or herself in an attempt to uproot irrational ideas or outdated beliefs. Dr. Maxie C. Maultsby, Jr. at the University of Kentucky Medical Center, calls his approach Rational Behavior Therapy (RBT) and his clients are encouraged to engage in deliberate self-analysis in an effort to identify and eliminate irrational ideas.

Dr. Maultsby says: "As he makes rational insights in therapy and applies them to an increasing number of situations, the client becomes an expert on his own behavior and can give himself corrective learning experiences at will. In effect, he becomes his own therapist—one of the main goals of rational therapy." RET therapists feel that if clients can learn to put their irrational thoughts into sentences, they can fairly easily formulate more rational sentences which will lead to more rational behavior. They believe many alcoholic people tend to over react, or "catastrophize" events because of a variety of misconceptions about the way life should be.

In his book, *A Guidebook for Alcoholics*, Drake Weston tells of his personal experiences in seeking help from AA, traditional psychotherapies, and finally, RET. He wrote, ". . . methods of AA have helped thousands . . . On the other hand, there are thousands of other people who have had little or no success with AA methods or procedures. In many such cases, an approach that is less on the spiritual and moral and more on the psychological and physiological side can be helpful." He notes that in insight therapy, one does a lot of talking about his alcoholism; but action is not a part of the plan. He advises, "Most importantly, do something."

A "cafeteria" plan for alcoholism treatment in which clients choose an individualized rehabilitation course from a variety of modalities, has been offered by the University of North Carolina. Dr. John A. Ewing, the plan's author, observed that treatment programs often offer a single philosophy approach, in spite of research findings that no one single approach is effective with all alcoholics. He believes that until more is known about matching patients with specific treatment programs, centers must offer a more comprehensive selection of options.

"Clinics which have broadened their therapeutic program by adopting such a concept have found that they can offer treatment to a larger number of patients and that attrition rates diminish," Dr. Ewing said to the 31st International Congress on Alcohol and Drug Dependence in Bangkok, Thailand.

His "cafeteria plan" divides the services into three groups. Group A includes support groups and education, medication, and for those who want it, Alcoholics Anonymous, family therapy, and insight therapies; Group B, includes behavior therapies and patient clubs; and Group C includes encounter groups, occupational therapy, rehabilitation programs, and psychodrama. Dr. Ewing believes each patient should be allowed to sample the variety offered on the therapeutic "menu" and pick what is right for himself.

Dr. Ewing reports that clinics which offer the "cafeteria plan" report fewer dropouts, better attendance, more interest, more family involvement, and better overall results. (For further information, contact him at the Center for Alcohol Studies, University of N.C., Chapel Hill, N.C. 27514.)

At the 3HO center in Tucson, Arizona, therapy for alcoholism is based on yoga techniques. Those associated with 3HO (which stands for the 3 Hs of "Happy, Healthy, and Holy" Organization) practice a special lifestyle of yoga based upon and including yoga exercises, meditation, and vegetarianism. (Meat eating, in yoga disciplines is associated with man's lower nature and with a craving for alcohol). The organization was founded by Yogi Bhajan. There are now about one hundred centers.

"Yoga and related natural, healing techniques such as meditation have been incorporated into a holistic approach to help clients achieve and maintain drug-free states," according to the director of the Tucson center, Sat Nam Singh. He says: "Yoga can aid in relieving stress from the physical body and helps calm the emotions, so that the individual can relax. Over time, the yoga helps bring about a healthy body and a positive alert mind."

Some of the clients in the residential and outpatient treatment program are addicted to heroin and other drugs but 50% or more have alcohol problems. Detoxification is achieved without the use of drugs. Clients receive massages and baths to promote relaxation, and a well-balanced vegetarian diet as well as other yoga activities. Clients are helped to break old habits and acquire a new chemical-free lifestyle. They report a success rate of about 50%. The program is divided into three phases: (1) clients are restricted to the premises; (2) they become involved in a selection of career training or continued education, and (3) they go through a process which begins the transition of going back into the community to live and work. (oFor further information write: Mukla Kaur Khalsa, 3HO Drug Abuse Prevention Center, 1050 N. Cherry Ave., Tucson, Ariz. 85719.)

In the New York and New Jersey areas, persons in need of detoxification can go to Mt. Carmel Hospital in Paterson, N.J. Many local companies send their liquor-soaked employees there for drying out and rehabilitation. This is one of the few hospitals in the US which is exclusively for alcoholics. Mt. Carmel admits approximately fifteen hundred patients a year for medical treatment and low-key psychological counseling. The reasonable cost is

$170 for five days and is usually paid by the overdrinker because, as a spokesman explained: "We want him to remember his last drunk—and what it cost him."

A single trip to Mt. Carmel is usually effective but the alcoholic is allowed to go there three times. "After that," explained the spokesman, "he strikes out." According to the National Council on Alcoholism, one out of every fourteen employees is an alcoholic. These are not skid row types but executives, white and blue color workers, family men and women, some Ph.D.s. The National Council estimates that compulsive drinking costs American Industry about $4.3 billion a year in absenteeism, sloppy work, wasted material, and the expense of training replacements; not to mention losses due to poor judgement on the part of top-level management.

The trend, over the years, has been away from the focus on the skid row overdrinker to the elite alcoholic: celebrities, executives, the well-educated and the well-to-do; such as officials in industry, the military, and in government. A recent newspaper article had the headline "Congress Riddled with Problem Drinkers." An executive whose brain is fuzzy with alcohol can lose his firm millions by an ill-advised merger. A politician can make a wrong decision affecting billions of people if his mind is beclouded with booze. One program that focuses only on executives and elite alcoholics was begun by Dr. William F. Hull, on "millionaire's row," in an exclusive and picturesque section of Southern California.

Dr. Hull is a clinical psychologist who has begun an alcohol treatment program called Halre Inc., based at Murrieta Hot Springs, Calif. He believes he has a cure for alcoholism and that the alcoholic may return to social drinking without harm. He says he has been treating problem drinkers in his medical practice for seventeen years and curing them. He first became interested in the problem in 1960, when several of his patients with anxiety problems reported that, after treatment, they had been able to drink moderately without a return to compulsiveness. Since they had not been treated for alcoholism, Dr. Hull felt something important was happening.

Halre Inc., is a privately operated, alcoholism rehabilitation center, offering a two week program for alcoholics in an atmosphere free of the stresses of everyday life. For this short program, clients are charged a flat fee of $4,000. Dr. Hull concedes it is a high price but maintains that the results are well worth the cost, and it is usually paid by the company. After undergoing his treatment, he says, the individual may no longer be said to be alcoholic. Dr. Hull does not believe that alcohol is the cause of alcoholism. during his studies, Dr. Hull discovered what he calls the "Panic-Suffocation Syndrome," which includes feelings of panic, helplessness, hopelessness, depression, mental exhaustion, rage and, most of all, a feeling of needing air. The syndrome, Dr. Hull says, is not only a common factor in alcoholics, but in drug addicts and persons who experience nervous breakdowns.

The Halre program attempts to remove this "Panic-Suffocation Syndrome," and when this happens, Dr. Hull says, the need to escape by means of alcohol no longer exists and so the desire for alcohol vanishes. When this is done, the individual, he says, is confident, relaxed, comfortable, and able to think more clearly. Dr. Hull maintains that a traumatic experience—usually after adolescence—combined with the use of alcohol, is what makes the individual predisposed to alcohol, rather than to drugs or to a nervous breakdown. He claims, as he gained experience in treating alcoholics, his success rate went from three out of ten to eight out of ten, and he expects it to go even higher. Dr. Hull invites Alcoholics Anonymous to send their failures to him. He says, "We can cure them."

In England, Dr. Douglas Cameron, psychiatrist at the Druiry Clinic, 50 Leicester Road, Narborough, Leicester, LE 9 5DF, London, England, has done a number of important studies on controlled drinking. His paper, "Lessons from an Outpatient Controlled Drinking Group," has been circulated widely in this country. (A charming aspect of this program is that, in certain instances, the therapist will go pub crawling with a patient, to help set up a pattern of moderation on the actual site of the mischief, so to speak.)

In France, the latest thing is therapeutic communities, whose major innovative feature is the incorporation of the parents and spouses of addicts into the therapeutic process. Therapeutic communities are being tried in such diverse locations as Malaysia, Sweden, Indonesia, Italy, and the Phillippines. Dr. Maxwell Jones, often considered to have founded the modern concept of the therapeutic communities at Henderson Hospital in London, is now working in the US. It is his belief that a crisis of identity resulting from the dehumanizing aspects of too many modern societies causes drug abuse.

chapter 7

On Psychological Dependence

In AA they speak of alcoholics as having a mental obsession with alcohol. The psychological model of alcoholism is based upon a wide range of psychoanalytic theories of personality. The various proponents of this model (such as Emrick, 1974) say that the psychodynamic theory of alcohol abuse rests upon one or a combination of three assumptions: (1) Alcoholism is a result of unconscious tendencies such as self-destruction, latent homosexuality, or fixation at the oral stage of development; (2) Alcoholism represents a need for power and autonomy; and (3) Alcoholism is related to repressed hostility and strong dependency needs.

While this view has its strong proponents, the evidence is inconclusive, and certain important questions have been raised including: "If the alcohol abuser exhibits dependency needs is this a result of his alcohol addiction or the cause of it?" Then, too, oral regression, suicidal tendencies, and homosexuality also occur in people who don't drink at all.

Psychiatrists have described alcoholic persons as neurotic, maladjusted, unable to effectively relate to others, sexually and emotionally immature, isolated, and dependent. They also say alcohol addicts are unable to withstand normal frustrations, are poorly integrated, and have feelings of "sinfulness" and "unworthiness." Unfortunately, there are no reliable studies to either confirm or deny these findings.

Researchers have gathered data to prove that alcoholic individuals come from broken homes or discordant ones, and that they have undergone heavy emotional deprivation in childhood. But many nonalcoholic persons have come from similar backgrounds and have similar personality traits. Perhaps some of the latter became criminals or mental patients; but some lead normal, reasonably happy lives. Reality factors, of course, have a bearing but they are not all of it. The following had mothers who didn't give a whoop for them, or fathers who were habitual drunkards:

George Bernard Shaw, H.G. Wells, Lord Byron, Percy Shelley, Charles Dickens, and Leonardo da Vinci.

Dr. Robert Knight depicted the alcoholic person as one who has difficulty in dealing with his or her deep sense of inferiority, inhibited aggressiveness and thwarted competitiveness. Dr. Harold Blane stressed that they are unable to reconcile feelings of worthlessness with omnipotent fantasies. Research conducted by William and Joan McCord indicates no single definable set of circumstances that necessarily predisposes an individual to alcoholism.

According to the late Dr. Karl Menninger: "Since it is true that alcohol has the quality of giving some degree of relief from the pain of facing reality and, also, from other psychic pain resulting from emotional conflicts, to the extent that it is sought for the purpose of relieving pain, the use of alcohol can be regarded as an attempt at self-cure." He says many alcoholics realize this; some feel that their sprees should be forgiven and not held against them. "The wish to be treated like a child and have one's most serious aggression overlooked," he says, "is very characteristic of the type of person who finds excessive indulgence in alcohol so irresistible." The reason for this, he believed, is not some perverse wickedness, but rather rooted in "the deep hopelessness and despair from which every alcoholic secretly suffers."

In Dr. Karen Horney's view, the alcoholic is an alienated individual in flight from his "real self." His alcoholic tendencies come from a loss of identity. He is remote from his beliefs, wishes and energies and he uses alcohol to allay anxiety and vindictive rage. Nothing is clear to him; like many neurotics who live in a fog, so the alcoholic seeks the haze of alcohol. Often people who have problems with thwarted aggressive feelings turn to alcohol to help them release pent up anger.

There is proof that liquor stimulates aggressive behavior in both humans and animals. In the laboratory this was demonstrated with Siamese Fighting Fish. These fish, bred for centuries, have brilliant coloring, long fins, and are very pugnacious. When alcohol was added to their water tank, they became even more vicious. Tests show that rats, too, become more aggressive under the influence of alcohol. Neurobiologist David Ingle poured the equivalent of two dozen martinis into a tank containing goldfish and after the fish were, in Dr. Ingle's words, "good and drunk" a number of tests were performed on them. "With a little alcohol, they learned faster and better, but with bigger doses they'd get depressed and didn't learn well . . . With more alcohol they suffer loss of memory, become aggressive, or lose all fear and judgement," said Dr. Ingle.

Alcohol has been cited as a contributing factor in suicides, automobile crashes, drownings, fatal accidents, fires, fights, murders, and plane crashes. According to Dr. Richard E. Boyatzis in the *Journal of Alcohol Studies*: "Although equipment malfunction and situational factors probably account for some of these, it is likely that human recklessness plays a major role." 'Human recklessness' may be considered another label for the type of high-risk assertive behavior often demonstrated by persons who have been drinking.

One view of alcoholism is that it is an attempt to regain a lost equilibrium. Another is that it is a means for the alcoholic to get other people to notice and take care of him: "a cry for help and attention." Dr. Rainaut of France, compares the drinker's retreat from reality to that of the LSD user who goes on a trip. He says: "The more he drinks, the more the alcoholic gets out of it, and the more difficult for anyone to reach him conversationally or any other way, expecially with a moral message."

While many investigators link alcoholism to the early, unfortunate childhood experiences of the drinker, one wonders what was it that predisposed the person to the choice of alcohol as the means to attempt to make his intolerable life more tolerable? One alcoholic described his childhood as "horrendous" and "terrifying." He said: "I find life a little less savage when I'm drinking; it takes the edge off of reality and makes it more dreamlike."

Karl Menninger's theory about alcoholics is as follows: "Such individuals, as children, have endured bitter disappointment, unforgiveable disappointment. They feel, and with justification, that they have been betrayed, and their entire subsequent life is a prolonged, disguised reaction to this feeling. It is true that every child meets with disappointment and frustration; this is inevitable in the nature of reality. . .In this respect, then, the alcoholic probably doesn't suffer in childhood anything qualitatively different from what the rest of us suffer; but, apparently, there is a quantitative difference. In the case of the alcoholic, the disappointment has actually been greater than he could bear."

Psychotherapy has been helpful to many alcoholics in achieving long lasting results in moderation or abstention. Psychotherapy involves self-examination, counseling, and guidance. A trained therapist works with, rather than on, patients, alone or in groups to help them explore feelings, attitudes and emotions, changing negative ones to those that are more rewarding. The therapy begins with the idea that the patient needs help and attempts to probe some of the underlying problems.

Therapy for alcoholic patients usually is somewhat different than that for other patients, with more emphasis on action and a focusing on the alcoholic's immediate life situation, rather than too much delving into early life history. The drinking must be stopped or brought under control, for much the same reason that the fire in a mattress must be smothered before taking the time to consider what caused the blaze. Some therapists bring in various members of the patient's family for counseling. Research has indicated that a family may include members that are even more emotionally disturbed than the overdrinker, containing a person, perhaps, who is literally driving the alcoholic to drink!

How long is treatment? It is difficult to say, different cases varying widely. Frequent sessions are suggested at the beginning of treatment, with sessions at longer intervals as time goes on. For a few it may go on for a lifetime, for most, a period of months is indicated and for some, a few years. short time therapy, such as is given by the Cleveland Center for Alcoholism, consists of from one to five therapeutic sessions. This very short time therapy was found to be most effective with alcoholics with good family ties, a determination to get well, and a willingness to face the situation quickly.

In his book, *Hooked People*, psychiatrist Dr. Lawrence J. Hatterer, writes: "Each of us feels the impact of addiction in some form, whether through family, friends, lovers, or simply the passing encounters with strangers. No day goes by without one's being bombarded by every media to engage in some excess, whether it is food, alcohol, drugs, sex, smoking, gambling, acquiring, or simply work itself . . . Addiction of one kind or another permeates every aspect of American life." (He notes that addictions are often complementary to one another, and people frequently move from one kind to another.)

Dr. Hatterer, who resides in New York City, says, "I've treated alcoholics for twenty-five years, and I, myself, have periodically been work-addicted, so I have some insight into that particular one." He thinks it is important to differentiate addiction from a habit. "A habit is something we may do almost every day, the same way we did it the day, week, month or year before." Habits can be good or bad. The World Health Organization defines an addiction as "a state of periodic or chronic intoxication detrimental to the individual and to society, produced by repeated consumption of a natural or synthetic drug and characterized by three factors: an overpowering compulsion to continue its use, and to obtain it by any means; a tendency to increase the dose, and a physical or psychologic dependency on the drug." Dr. Hatterer says the behavior is always initially experienced as pleasurable, but ultimately is without sustained gratification. Yet it has served a purpose in the addict's life. "When we use the addictive activity to cope with isolation, when everything and everyone around us becomes too ugly to endure, when we lose touch with people, or lose the ability to feel . . . the addiction can become the only reward we give ourselves to ease the pain of failure or rejection."

Dr. Hatterer believes the old concept of analysis as the psychiatrist sitting around and listening to the patient for years is pretty much gone. "It's gone for a number of reasons," he says: "results left something to be desired and the cost was too much both in terms of time, psychic energy, and money. It treated the patient as if he lived in a vacuum."

Says Dr. Hatterer: "More people want help and can't afford the expense and time of the drawn-out process. So, on a purely pragmatic level—group therapy, family therapy, marital therapy, encounter therapy—all these enable you to reach more people. They are accelerated ways of helping certain people—but not all." He has patients who need to go into groups because they need socialization and other patients who require family therapy situations in which you must bring in the entire family.

Dr. Hatterer compares the artist and the homosexual to the addict; because they are all considered by society as deviants: "marching to the beat of a different drummer." All are somewhat "outsiders" to the mainstream of society. The artist, he says, comments on society, the addict is a dropout, and the homosexual has rejected heterosexuality in favor of another lifestyle. (He says labeling the artist, addict, and homosexual as deviants is not done in a critical sense but to help understand their special problems in relation to the rest of society.)

"Alcoholics, generally, have more in common with each other than just their alcoholism," wrote Mrs. Marty Mann: "It has been noted time and again, that alcoholism all too frequently strikes the 'most promising' member of a family, a school class or a business

. . . the alcoholic very often seems to be . . . a little more intelligent than his fellows in their particular social, economic or vocational level. This may well be the result of an unusual sensitivity, also widely noted by students and researchers, similar to that attributed to creative people."

Dr. Hatterer believes that when the compulsion—the drinking, eating, taking drugs or whatever—becomes not only a physical or a psychologic craving, but our very "emotional life's blood," the individual has become an addict. This is the stage where the dose has to be periodically increased. "Then we have reached the point of no return when our minds and bodies aren't having fun with it anymore; it has taken charge of us."

Dr. Hatterer tape-records every session with his patients and has found it useful to let them edit the tape of the session. "Patients who are motivated to treatment will study the tapes and learn from them," he says. "Those that are resistant to treatment will lose the tapes, forget to bring them back, or in some other way sabotage the treatment." (He gains insight into patients by their attitude toward the tapes.) He believes this tape confrontation considerably speeds up the therapeutic process.

Dr. Hatterer does joint therapy and has been doing it for ten years: "I have couples come in and discuss their problems, fight their fights, and I make certain interpretations. They take that tape home and they listen to the confrontation of themselves, often to their great enlightenment." As he finds patients getting better, they no longer have a need to listen to the tapes, because they are feeling better: "If the headache is gone, why bother taking aspirin?"

While being analytically trained, Dr. Hatterer uses anything he can to get insight into his patients: dreams, fantasies, patient's history, position in society, value system, interpersonal transactions, etc. Many of his patients are creative people such as designers, artists, poets, etc. Quite a few have overcome drinking problems.

chapter 8

Is There an Alcoholic Personality?

In the traditional literature on alcoholism, we find the picture of the alcoholic personality anything but a pretty one. Though its findings are inconclusive, it is remarkably consistent. Researchers Machover and Puzzo (1959) administered a battery of tests to forty-six alcoholics. They found homosexual trends, female identification, and sex role ambivalence. "Schizoidness" was attributed to almost all the alcoholics, along with general passivity, a strict superego, and orality.

In a study by Halpern (1946), a pattern of emotional disturbance was found, but no distinctive pattern other than "does not withdraw from disturbing situations." Halpern reported finding a normal amount of masculinity on vocational interest, but there was a tendency for the alcoholics to overestimate what they could do. According to Dr. William R. Miller: "If alcoholics have any personality in common, it would be 'psychopathic deviance.'" This may include depression, hysteria, paranoia, or mania.

According to Hewitt (1943), "alcoholic addiction . . . seems to be associated, with but few exceptions, with deep personality disorders." Other traits attributed to the alcoholic person have been dependency, neuroticism, and narcissism. Dr. Miller states: "One could conclude, from this research, the average alcoholic is passive, overactive, inhibited, acting out, and withdrawn: a gregarious psychopath with a conscience, defending against poor defenses as a result of excessive or insufficient mothering."

In a study at the Katherine Hamilton Mental Health Center, Terre Haute, Ind., alcoholic persons exhibited a much higher incidence of pathological depression than abusers of other drugs. They recommended that the factor of depression should always be considered when therapy is being planned for alcohol abusers. The study focused on forty-two patients at the center, twenty-one diagnosed as alcohol abusers and twenty-one as abusers of other drugs. The researchers stressed the need for alcohol abusers to learn coping skills. They added: "Counseling techniques that focus on handling day-to-day stress and understanding personal aggressions and resentments would be most helpful."

In a film titled *The Sad and Sorry Life of Billy Be Damned*, eight major psychological factors which contribute to alcoholism among the American Indian are identified as : (1) desire to escape, (2) wish to attain identity, (3) poor self-image, (4) anger, (5) loneliness, (6) fantasy, (7) disappointment, and (8) no guilt or shame over drinking.

Studies have shown that a person is a high-risk to become a problem drinker if there is a family history of alcoholism or teetotalism, where there is an unstable family life, where there was an absentee or rejecting father or mother, or being the last child of a large family; or with a history of depression or heavy smoking. (Heavy drinking is often associated with heavy smoking, but the reverse need not be true.)

Dr. Robert Knight, in 1940, depicted the person most likely to become an alcoholic as one in whom "there is repressed, but still active cravings for loving, maternal care." Karl Menninger wrote, in 1938, that many alcoholics were depressed people, who use alcohol as a means of hopefully allaying depression. He wrote: "Alcoholics have a strong need to destroy themselves, because of guilt and a need for punishment caused by personally unacceptable aggressive impulses." He noted, "drinking performs two functions psychologically, a gradual form of self-destruction, satisfying the need for punishment, and acts as a substitute for a more greatly feared act: suicide."

Noting the similarity between alcoholics and drug abusers, Sandor Rado, writing in 1926, wrote: "Addicts are persons who have a disposition to react to drugs in a specific way, namely in such a way that they try to use their effects to satisfy the archaic oral longing, which is a sexual longing, a wish for security, and a need to maintain self-esteem."

Environmental influences play a very important role in determining drinking behavior of course. Freud and others brought home the idea that behavior has meaning and significance and can be understood. While the Freudian emphasis on early childhood experiences as predetermining later actions may seem somewhat fatalistic, it frequently has validity. The Freudians believed alcohol was used as a pacifier for infantile longings and the symbolic gratification of maternal succor. Also they believed that alcohol was used to deal with latent homosexual strivings and to resolve the conflicts of dependence and passivity.

An American-Danish research team reported a strong hereditary association with alcoholism in 1973. The researchers reported in the *Archives of General Psychiatry*: "The data indicate that children of alcoholics are more likely to have alcohol problems than are children of nonalcoholics, despite being separated from their alcoholic parent early in life. The role of heredity in alcoholism has been hotly debated for years. Dr. E.M. Jellinek reported, years ago, that out of a total of 4,372 alcoholics, at least 52% had an alcoholic parent. Rather than a "predisposing gene," he felt the predisposing factor might be being born into an environment that fosters alcoholic behavior. Others believe an inherited biochemical defect could affect the brain.

Many psychologists see alcoholism as a form of emotional illness joined to an addiction. The person was emotionally troubled to begin with, so goes this theory. This trouble made the drinker develop certain character traits, such as emotional and sexual immaturity, strong dependency needs, feelings of inadequacy, inability to tolerate tension, and extreme sensitivity, hostility, and insecurity. Dr. David C. McClelland of Harvard wrote in *Psychology Today*: "The excessive drinker is the man with an excessive need for personal power who has chosen drinking as the way to accentuate his feeling of power."

In a study by the Medical Foundation, conducted at Brookline, Mass., of young alcohol and drug abusers it was reported that the abusers were much more likely (than non-abusers) to come from single-parent homes, score poorly on their studies, be less able to talk to patents, be less religious, to have psychiatric help, and to feel they have more problems than their friends. They were more generally alienated from society.

"Alcoholism is but one of a number of ways of dealing with life's stresses and is best regarded as a symptom of such maladaptation," says Dr. Anthony Reading, of Johns Hopkins hospital. He believes the psychological factors associated with alcoholism include: low frustration tolerance, excessive dependency and needs (sometimes masked as pseudo-independence), underlying feelings of inferiority and self-doubt. Many alcoholics fear rejection and have trouble entering into any but superficial social relationships. They are also very sensitive to rejection.

He says: "A great many alcoholic patients are extremely pleasant and agreeable when sober, on the surface at least. Nice people, such as these, often have a long history of difficulty in actively expressing feelings of anger or frustration for fear of possible consequences. When sober, they may have no outlet for such feelings except more passive and indirect routes (such as missing an appointment or being late), and unless this process is recognized, it can serve to infuriate those who are trying to be helpful."

He believes that while certain psychodynamic, personality, and psychosocial factors are clearly associated with alcoholism, none is sufficient to explain it because these typical predisposing factors are not invariably present in all alcoholic persons and, moreover, are also found in nonalcoholic persons. According to *Keller's Law*, "the investigation of any trait in alcoholics will show that they either have more or less of it," or, stated differently: "Alcoholics are different in so many ways that it makes no difference."

Here are a few examples from Mark Keller's list of oddities of alcoholics that is too long to reproduce in full: "Alcoholics are (as compared with other populations) more allergic, less bald, more first born, less introverted, more color-blind, less socialized, more dependent, less responsible, more alcohol tolerant, less tolerant to frustration, more accident-prone, less religiously tolerant, less hypnotizable, more amnesiac, more drug-consuming, less conditionable, more suicidal, less married, more incarcerated, less feminine (women), more effeminized (men), less potent (men), more frigid (women), less prosperous, more impulsive, more rigid, less self-sex-image secure, more depressed, more sociopathic, less fecund, more rejected, less treatable, more imaginative, and more thirsty . . . ."

Harold T. Blane introduced what he called: "The Three D's of alcoholism: (1) Dependency, (2) Depression (in drinkers resulting from an unsuccessful wish for maternal love during childhood), and (3) Denial—of depression, dependency, and the drinking problem. Dr. Blane says many alcoholics are unable to tolerate frustration or control instincts and impulses. Another doctor described some alcoholics as having "an ominous impulsivity." Even though the person is not drinking, he may be accused of going on 'dry' drunks, which is getting into the frame of mind usually associated with spree drinking, without the use of booze.

The trouble with the view of the alcoholic personality, as described by traditionalists, is that many of these traits appear in nonalcoholics and do not in all alcoholics. Moreover, some persons seem to have some of these traits, at one point in time, but not in another. Some alcoholics appear to take a "flight into health from treatment"—and may indeed "get it all together"—and become mature, self-reliant, and independent people in control of their drinking and their lives.

The traditional view also makes the point that a person's social, vocational, and economic situation is of no importance. The researcher Gerard, for example believes that excessive drinking is simply one dimension of a responsibility-avoiding lifestyle. Dr. Donald Finlay has written, "It is a lifestyle characterized by a failure to take responsibility for one's actions and programs should be addressed to this." (One has to consider whether it is more to the point to say, it's a nonconformist lifestyle.)

Some believe the alcoholic is simply more sensitive than others and is thus driven to drink. The pressures of modern life are having an adverse effect on many people. Dr. Philip G. Zimbardo, professor of psychology at Stanford University, has a very pessimestic view of the effect of crowded, modern cities on the human psyche, believing it is driving many to extremes of behavior. He cites the sharp increase in murders in recent years, the increase in child abuse, and the wave of recent assassinations. The increase in alcoholism may be related to a turning inward of tensions, hostility, and anxiety, the alcohol being used as a pacifier for rage.

"What we are observing all around us," says Dr. Zimbardo, "is a sudden change in the restraints which normally control the expression of our drives, impulses, and emotions." Dr. Zimbardo suggests that what is happening is that many of the old restraints in American life, imposed by such institutions as the large family, are being dissolved by a process he calls "deindividuation." Conditions which foster "deindividuation," he says, "make each of us potential assassins."

In a recent interview, Dr. Zimbardo suggested that the sheer size of many American cities, the feeling of powerlessness in the face of big institutions, the widespread renting of apartments, rather than the owning of houses, and the immense mobility of Americans were among the factors that appeared to lead toward a weakening of controls, based on self-evaluation. And what drives some to be assassins drives others, more passive, to drink. If a David Berkowitz (accused of killing seven in New York and wounding many others) had taken to drink, turning his aggression inward instead of outward in sociopathetic behavior, one wonders if many lives would have been saved.

Surely, are not such factors as inflation, high unemployment, increased divorce rate, corruption in government, depersonalization, increased taxation, overcrowding, scarcity of inexpensive food, lodging, and clothing more responsible for alcoholism than any inborn personality traits?

A study done for the US Congressional Joint Committee suggests a statistical link between high unemployment and increased rates of alcoholism, mental illness, suicide, homicide and other strong indicators of sociological stress. The study was done by M. Harvey Brenner, Ph.D. Associate Professor, Johns Hopkins University. Senator Hubert Humphrey, Chairman of the Committee, said, "the report suggests that even a 1.4% increase in unemployment, during 1970 alone, was associated with some fifteen hundred additional suicides; seventeen hundred additional homicides; twenty-five thousand additional strokes, heart, and kidney deaths; fifty-five hundred additional mental hospital admissions and eight hundred additional deaths from cirrhosis of the liver . . ."

Brenner's comprehensive study embraced the period from the Depression through the 1970s. He said: "Additional findings continued to reflect the importance of the inverse relationship between consumption of distilled spirits and the state of the national economy . . . Arrests for drunkenness in Massachusetts, for instance, were found to be inversely related to the national economy 1915–1968, with arrests lagging two years behind fluctuations in the economy." Finally, "arrest rates for driving while intoxicated in the US as a whole . . . were definitely found to increase substantially during the national economic recession."

As metals have different degrees of pressure that they can withstand, so people have individual breaking points. This breaking point may have more to do with the amount of pressure put on the person rather than his innate character structure. Accusing the deviant of being completely at fault is a cop-out. Alcoholics are made, not born. It has never been proven they are flawed with any uniform character defect, except possibly an over-appreciation of the effects of alcoholic spirits.

chapter 9

On Physiological Craving

It has long been a basic tenet of traditional alcohologists that there exists a strong physiological craving for alcohol that can be triggered by one drink. This gives rise to the AA slogan, "One drink, drunk." The available research does not support this notion of loss-of-control. A number of scientific researchers have reported over a number of years that even when provided with priming doses of alcohol, either surreptitiously or openly, chronic alcoholics are not induced into uncontrolled drinking, even if more alcohol is available to them. The fact is many alcoholics terminate their drinking with no problems.

A most interesting experiment, in this regard, was conducted in 1973 by Marlatt, Demming, and Reid. A group of both alcoholics and social drinkers were provided with beverages to consume. Half the subjects in the group were led to believe that the beverages contained alcohol, while the other half were led to believe that the beverages were nonalcoholic. The results indicated that the amount that the alcoholics consumed was highly related to what they were told rather than to the actual content of the beverage. Thus, if they were told they were drinking alcohol, whether they were or not, they consumed more of the beverage. The amount of the beverage consumed was not influenced, even if he was drinking alcohol, if the alcoholic believed he was drinking a nonalcoholic beverage.

In a study of the Alcoholism Research Unit in Baltimore City Hospitals, the alcoholics who were promised a reward for moderation were able to stop after five drinks or fewer. The subjects were nineteen chronic hospitalized alcoholics. All were told that they could have one ounce drinks whenever they asked for them with a limit of twenty-four ounces. On certain days the alcoholics were offered no incentive for not drinking too much. On other days they were told that if they restricted their intake to five ounces or less, they could work in the laundry (and earn $1.00 per hour), take part in group therapy, have visitors, chat with other patients, use the game rooms, and watch TV or play pool.

The results were very interesting. On the no-reward days, almost all the patients drank too much. On the reward days, every one of these chronic alcoholics proved he could control his drinking to within the five ounce limit or abstain. The amazing thing, to the researchers, was the absolute consistency of the results, proving to them, at least, that abstinence or drunkenness are not the only alternatives for the alcoholic. (Behaviorists had long before begun to question the validity of the belief that no alcoholic can learn to moderate his or her drinking.) If you make it worth their while, many can indeed gain control over their habits.

The idea that there exists two kinds of drinkers, social drinkers and alcoholics, and that the latter is a "different breed of cat," has also not been proven. Although there have been a number of research studies, it has been a blind alley in discovering any physical basis as the cause of overdrinking. In a report from NIAAA it said in part . . . "neither chemicals in specific beverages nor physiological, nutritional, metabolic, nor genetic defects have been found which could explain alcoholic drinking."

A Canadian Cooperative Commission on the Study of Alcoholism says that only 1% of alcohol users eventually reach a state that could be called addiction and that "it requires large amounts, several thousand times more than morphine, heroin, or barbiturate addiction over a long period of time ranging from three to twenty years." This, of course, disputes those AA members who claim to be alcoholics from the very first time they picked up a drink.

To quote again from the Canadian Commission: "The inability to abstain is not an all-or-nothing thing; that is, individuals with this condition do not always become intoxicated once they begin to drink again. Many alcohol addicts have no problem with abstention in a protected setting such as a hospital, jail, or nursing home, but once controls have been lifted, they have difficulty." Thus, true rehabilitation, for these people, must produce a change of attitudes and the replacement of external controls (police, courts, prison, locked hospital wards) with conscious inner controls—and this necessitates a desire to change. The problem, then, is one of motivation rather than body chemistry or being possessed by the "Demon Rum."

The loss-of-control, or physiological craving, was held for decades as a basic concept of the disease model of alcoholism. If this is untrue, the disease concept collapses. But as Dr. Peter Miller has said, "It remains, however, not for the disease concept to be disproven, but for someone to present concrete evidence for its existence. At this point in time, it seems unwise to take a firm stand in favor of such a model when there is no evidence to support it and, indeed, an increasing number of reports refuting it."

Of course the position of AA is that alcoholism is a physical allergy plus mental obsession. Mrs. Mary Mann has stated: "Alcoholics apparently have something in their makeup which causes them to react to alcohol differently than other people, something for which the word allergy is at least an understandable term, and that this condition is what makes it impossible for them ever to drink, since there is no known cure." Other AA members have also claimed a physiological distinction for the alcoholic: "It seems likely that an individual is an alcoholic before he ever picks up the first drink."

But a number of studies, including those of Drs. Mark and Linda Sobell have concluded beyond a reasonable doubt that persons with alcohol problems do not experience physical dependence merely from consuming small amounts of alcohol following a period of abstinence. The Bon Accord Program in Ontario, Canada, did a study of ninety chronic alcoholics of the skid row type in hospital residence. These alcoholics were given the choice of abstinence or controlled drinking. Results indicated that the men were well able to control their drinking.

According to Morton S. Propper, MSW, "An example of the blatant disregard for scientific findings in the alcoholism treatment field is the belief that one drink triggers an uncontrollable urge in the alcoholic to keep on drinking." A study by A. Parades confirmed that it does not. Similar findings have been the result in twenty other previously published studies. J. Mendelson, the first chief of the National Center for the Prevention and Control of Alcoholism, reported from experimental work that there is no evidence of any such "biological triggering effect."

Also, the work of D. Cahalan showed that many men with serious drinking problems are able to change their drinking habits and, so to speak, "mature out" of alcoholic drinking, even without therapeutic intervention. His study showed also that a large proportion of men in their twenties with serious alcohol problems have a high rate of "maturing out" (or spontaneous remission) in their early thirties.

Pattison pointed out that Dr. E.M. Jellinek's famous chart of alcoholic deterioration was based on a biased sample of all male AA members who were already physically and socially bankrupt.

As Dr. Jellinek himself commented of AA: "As I have said before AAs have naturally created the picture of alcoholism in their own image and likeness."

Most researchers today unanimously agree addiction is not purely a physiological mechanism. There is no proof that alcoholism is a unitary phenomena causing the alcoholic to be intrinsically different from the nonalcoholic, nor that continued drinking over a period of years necessarily leads to moral, physical, and social deterioration and/or death.

Aubrey J. Yates has written in his work, *Theory and Practise in Behavior Therapy*: "Considerable light has been thrown on the classical loss-of-control hypothesis . . . which makes three basic assertions about alcoholics: (1) The alcoholic is unable to resist drinking in the presence of others who are drinking, (2) The alcoholic will always drink if alcohol is available and (3) If the alcoholic takes a single drink, physiological changes will occur that will compel him to take another drink."

This loss-of-control theory, if true, says Yates, has two important implications: the aim of treatment must be total abstinence, and it is impossible to train an alcoholic to become a social drinker. He notes: "It is necessary to emphasize that this hypothesis is very widely accepted; and any suggestion that it may be false produces a state bordering on apoplexy among medical experts on alcoholism." He finds that: "Nevertheless, behavior analysis has provided very strong evidence that all three major propositions of the loss-of-control hypothesis are false," citing the work of Gottheil, Alterman, Skoloda, and Murphy (1973). Marlatt, Demming, and Reid (1973) also showed the relation of the drinking-rate as a function of *expectancy*.

Yates says in summary: "It is clear that careful behavior analytic studies have already paid a handsome dividend in the study of the behavior patterns of alcoholics. They have demonstrated that alcoholics do not necessarily lose control of their drinking as soon as they imbibe one drink, that they do not succeed in reducing anxiety and depression by drinking, that they do not necessarily drink to enable them to socialize more successfully, and that their drinking patterns are not quite what they are commonly believed to be. Some myths have been dispelled, or should have been, (beliefs about alcoholics, which are often heavily influenced by moral judgements about the evils of alcohol, die hard) . . . which have obvious implications for treatment that are already being put into effect."

Yet a punitive, moralistic attitude on the part of many workers in treatment facilities still persists. Some facilities will drop a patient if he is heard to be "drinking." One facility demands a urine specimen of alcoholics; and if this is refused, the patient will be dropped. These "unmotivated people," many of us believe, should not be dropped from treatment for drinking.

Taking into consideration all the evidence, all the AA stories one hears about an AA going berserk because of tasting the rum in a rum cake or putting some alcohol on his or her face must be attributed to pure imagination, fantasy, or some psychological quirk. Tasting the vanilla extract in a cake need not send an alcoholic off on a bender, unless the person is looking for just such an excuse.

In a study, in 1968, M.M. Glatt proposed that the loss-of-contol mechanism could not be triggered by one or two drinks, but rather by achieving a specific blood-alcohol concentration threshold, which would vary widely among drinkers. In other words, if this threshold were not surpassed, there would never be a loss-of-control. In a recent study, reported by Alfonso Parades, on a number of gamma alcoholics who had been abstinent for two weeks prior, drinking was confined to 0.14 blood alcohol level. None of the subjects (who previously had) experienced any loss-of-control. (And note that this is above the legal definition of drunkenness which is 0.10.) A study by Keller, in 1972, also indicated that no craving would appear until a certain blood alcohol level had been achieved. "Loss-of-control does not occur even in gamma alcoholics, unless the drinker is well into a drinking bout." This suggests that by monitoring their blood-alcohol level and not going beyond the cut off point, all drinkers could avoid ever experiencing any loss-of-control.

In the nutritional approach to alcoholism, a desire for alcohol is related to blood sugar levels. Dr. Roger Williams has pointed out that each person has a distinctive biochemical makeup. Some persons, for example, will appear intoxicated with an alcohol content in their blood of .05 percent; while another might appear sober with as much as eight times that. People are by no means alike physiologically and in their reactions to alcohol. Thus, each person who drinks should find out for himself or herself what he or she can or cannot do. Dr. Williams commented further: "It is scientifically unsound to suppose that what one can do, another can duplicate. And conversely, what one cannot do, another may be able to accomplish." Socrates had the right idea when he said: "Know thyself."

chapter 10

Alcohol and Drugs:

Special Dangers

Alcohol is the socially approved anesthesia of our time. Pharmacologically, alcohol is an anesthetic, not a stimulant. Indirectly, in small amounts, it seems to stimulate because it inhibits those centers of the brain which restrict our not so civilized impulses. It tends to make us more emotionally free to express ourselves, for better or for worse. With increasing doses, however, it puts to sleep the brain areas which affect judgment, memory, and control over our behavior. Given enough, it could put you to sleep forever!

Why do people voluntarily want to take an anesthetic to drug themselves? The reasons are complex and multiple, even a little mysterious. Some people overdrink because they can't stand the pain of living, whether that comes from external or internal causes. One alcoholic said, "I'm punch-drunk from too many whacks in the face in the prize ring of life." The cumulative pain from all the blows requires an anesthetic, according to this sad man. We are all familiar with the term "feeling no pain" in regard to drinking.

Our society teaches us from the cradle up that pain is something to be escaped from. When we go to the dentist, we are given an anesthetic. Our childhood operations were done under such pain killers as gas, ether, sodium pentathol, or others. (It would be interesting if a study were made of how many persons, who later became overdrinkers, had multiple childhood operations under anesthesia.)

When these people grow up and hurt again, as alcohol is legal and reasonably priced, they reach for this pain killer, as self-medication, to anesthetize psychic pain and to insulate themselves from an anxiety ridden world. And addiction being a cumulative thing, it is easy to pass from use, to abuse, to addiction.

An addict's life is not a happy one, whether his bag is alcohol or drugs. An addict's life operates on a crisis-to-crisis basis. It's a hectic, trauma-filled existence where every day is filled with big or little tragedies. He's hanging on the window ledge of life with nervous fingers.

We call it cross-dependence when a person is into alcohol and some other drug, such as barbiturates or tranquilizers, in an attempt to control anxiety. Such persons who seek mixed, pharmacological highs are playing with fire. Reports say that more persons die every year from mixing alcohol and drugs than in alcohol-related car accidents.

While mixing drugs and alcohol is a deadly business, substituting drugs for alcohol involves another risk. According to Rev. Jeffrey A. Dubron, a spokesman for the National Alliance on Alcoholism Prevention and Treatment (NAAPT): "Too often the physician or psychiatrist knows nothing of the correct treatment of alcoholism and so resorts to extreme use of pills to handle the problem. Studies conducted over the past two years have shown that an alcoholic seeking help for alcoholism may find himself given electric shock treatments or large doses of drugs leading to drug addiction. We have received testimony from doctors that quite often an alcoholic becomes addicted to pills that were given as a treatment for the alcohol problem. This compounds the problem in that before you can get to the root of the alcoholism, you must now contend with handling drug addiction."

From studies of that organization, he concludes that alcoholics profit most from nondrug treatment and a program of personal counseling. NAAPT functions under the injunction: "only the increase of trust and self-respect will help the alcoholic." Rev. Dubron cites the fact that the ethics committees of both the American Medical Association (AMA) and the American Psychiatric Association (APA) have not acted in a way to handle the vast reliance on drugs by both doctors and psychiatrists, noting that "a stream of dangerous drugs is still being given to alcoholics."

Says Dr. Ross Fishman, director of education and training for the National Council on Alcoholism, New York City's Affiliate: "The people we don't usually think about as dual drug abusers are the parents . . . and probably many housewives who regularly take prescription drugs and drink." He notes that: "With young people, we're talking about a shift from drugs alone to drugs plus alcohol."

Some experts believe the dual abuse of booze and pills is a product of a drug oriented society where young people are accustomed to seeing Mommy or Daddy (or both) taking prescriptions and drinking as a matter of custom and habit. Of course everyone is glad that teens have rejected hard drugs such as heroin, but mixing drugs and pills is also very dangerous.

There is a case of one boy in Boston who got booze and pills at a bar and some heroin at a party. By 4:00 A.M., nobody could wake him up or hear his heartbeat. Doctors did get his heart going again, but problems began with his kidneys, liver, and lungs. A tracheotomy was performed. For awhile his life was supported by only a heart-lung machine. The doctors began to worry about brain damage, if indeed, he would ever come out of the coma. Now the only outward sign of the ordeal is the tracheotomy scar on his throat and a certain breathlessness when he exercises. Unfortunately, he apparently hasn't learned his lesson. He says he still takes booze and pills "for recreation and in moderation." (Next time he ODs, he may not be so lucky.)

So parents and teens, be warned in regard to the deadly duo: alcohol and drugs. Combining booze with downers can lead to euphoria, coma, or death. One has only to remember the long continuing seige of eighteen-year-old Karen Quinlan, in a New Jersey hospital, who allegedly took an overdose of two popular American drugs: gin and tonic and the tranquilizer Valium. (You will remember her parents went to court to try to have her respirator unplugged, because of irreparable brain damage.) While the Quinlan case is admittedly extreme, people who are experimenting with any barbiturates, sedatives, and tranquilizers should avoid using alcohol, and vice-versa.

Alcohol and downers are both central nervous system depressants. They can stop the heartbeat, reduce blood pressure, and stem the supply of oxygen to the brain. One drug can magnify the effect of another. This "synergistic" effect means that even a less-than-lethal dose of alcohol plus a less-than-lethal dose of barbiturates could cause death.

Experts see dual use of alcohol and drugs as a way people try to cope with stress in a drug-oriented society. (Such slogans as "Better Living Through Chemistry" are constantly before us.) Says Judy Rich of New York's Accept Alcoholism Program: "Parents need to tune in to their own values about drinking and pill taking, before they can expect their kids not to take them." Drug industry sources say sleep aids alone, of the over-the-counter variety, had sales last year estimated at $34.2 million. Sleep aids often contain two ingredients widely used which have a potentially high toxicity:

bromides and scopalamine. (It is estimated that there are some five hundred thousand brand name drug products sold each year in the United States over-the-counter.)

But experts agree that addiction resides more in the addicted than in the agent. True physical dependence and "tolerance" (after repeated doses, there is a decrease in effect or larger and larger doses are required to get the same initial effect), occurs primarily with two classes of drugs, both of which are central nervous system depressants: narcotic analgesics and general anesthetics. The first group includes heroin, morphine, and other alkaloids of the poppy family. The second is made up of sedatives, hypnotics, sleeping potions, general anesthetics, and ethyl alcohol. But the trouble is not simply in the substance.

As Junius Adams points out in his book *Drink To Your Health*: "The alcoholic is an addictive personality, someone with an urge to be dependent, and alcohol just happens to be the substance he has chosen for his dependency. Alcohol, itself, does not cause dependency. The physical effects of drinking can usually be prevented or cured by vitamin-mineral therapy plus good nutrition. The desire to drink destructively is not inevitably connected to alcohol. Alcohol addicts could have chosen to become drug addicts, or addicted to gambling, over-eating, or criminality. The problem is: how to cure the *desire* to be dependent.

According to Stanton Peele and Archie Brodsky, writing in their book, *Love and Addiction*: "Addiction is not a chemical reaction. Addiction is an *experience*, one which grows out of an individual's routinized, subjective response to something that has special meaning for him—something, anything, that he finds so safe and reassuring that he cannot be without. So, if we want to come to terms with addiction, we have to stop pointing the finger at drugs and start looking at people, at ourselves, at what makes us dependent. We will find that we learn habits of dependence, in part, by growing up in a culture which teaches a sense of personal inadequacy, a reliance on external bulwarks, and a preoccupation with the negative or painful rather than the positive or joyous."

The addict sometimes becomes quite skilled in changing his crutch and, more than ever, today people tend to switch around. Interestingly, according to the Marihuana Commission: "Study after study which the Commission reviewed invariably reported an association between the use of tobacco and, to a lesser extent, of alcohol with the use of marihuana and other drugs . . . the overwhelming majority of marihuana users, however, do not progress to other drugs. They either remain with marihuana or foresake its use in favor of alcohol."

Marihuana has also been substituted in small amounts for alcohol by some people who believe it is safer than alcohol. This is not advised, however, as alcoholics are persons who have shown an inability to moderate their drug use and there are numerous reports of a tendency to shift their dependency to other drugs. Yet "drug therapy, while rarely recommended by physicians, is frequently prescribed," as noted by the Sobells. Psychoactive drugs, including tranquilizers, antidepressants, and sedatives constitute one of the most common therapys and it is estimated that 50% of all patients receive them. (These drugs are used as an adjunct to therapy and not a substitute for it, however.)

Valium and Librium are said to help in relieving withdrawal symptoms. Other compounds employed by physicians are sedative, hypnotic, or anesthetic substitutes for alcohol. In the 1950s, hallucinogenic compounds like LSD were given, not to treat a specific disorder, but to facilitate emotional release in psychotherapy. Some physicians see no harm in prescribing minor tranquilizers such as meprobate as a bridge from booze excesses to another way of life. Meprobate helps produce relaxation and freedom from tension.

The use of lithium as a therapeutic agent in the treatment of alcoholism has been investigated by Dr. N.S. Kline and others. Dr. Kline found it is valuable for some alcoholic patients with depression where it appears to modify the patients' drinking habits significantly. In a double-blind study, with the medication and placebo, of the patients who had to be readmitted for their drinking, researchers found the lithium group had fewer episodes as compared to the control group. Lithium appears to have a marked and statistically significant beneficial effect on chronic alcoholism with depression. Lithium also is one of the medications which can be safely administered for long periods of time. (The literature contains descriptions of studies in man which have been ongoing for fifteen years.)

It was René Descartes who stated that emotions are the expression of psychological processes which can be controlled by chemical agents. Such drugs as Thorazine, antidepressants like Elavil, and antianxiety drugs like Valium or Librium are widely asked for by patients as they offer some relief to disorganized thinking and other symptoms. Indeed, there are those who believe we are coming dangerously close to being a pharmacological society, with most everyone drugged to some extent (whether legally, by prescription, or on alcohol or small doses of marihuana or, illegally, on the hard drugs.) Patients in mental hospitals are kept on antipsychotic drugs like Thorazine to aid in custodial care. Some alcoholics are given Antabuse as a protective drug to keep them from drinking.

It was back in the early 1950s that disulfiram (Antabuse) first appeared on the alcoholism treatment scene. The drug, by making the user very sick if he takes any alcohol while on it, can enforce abstinence on some patients. Some programs such as probation, courts, etc., have made disulfiram treatment mandatory for chronic alcohol abusers. They hope that the enforced period of abstinence will help clear the brain and give the alcoholic a chance to get started on a drug free life. The abuser takes his white Antabuse pill once a day, and, thus, makes a chemical commitment to abstinence.

According to Ayerst Laboratories, US manufacturers of Antabuse, the alcohol-Antabuse reaction can be described as follows: "Antabuse plus alcohol, even in small amounts, produces flushing, throbbing head and neck, headache, respiratory difficulty . . . nausea, copious vomiting, sweating, thirst, chest pain, palpitation, difficulty breathing, very rapid heartbeat, hypertension, fainting . . . marked uneasiness, weakness, vertigo, blurred vision, and confusion. In severe reactions there may be respiratory depression, cardiovascular collapse, irregular heartbeat, myocardial infarction, acute congestive heart failure, unconsciousness, convulsions, and death." Some patients who were not drinking have reported skin disorders, drowsiness and impotence reactions, indicating that it has its own toxicity.

Because there is a strong possibility that Antabuse users will discontinue treatment, there is a growing interest on the part of some members of the alcoholism establishment to use Antabuse implants on alcoholic persons, which would sensitize them to alcohol for a period of six months. In this surgical operation, an incision is made and the Antabuse is implanted under the skin in the lower abdomen. A local anesthetic is used. In the words of Dr. Weisman, Antabuse users make "a symbolic and realistic commitment to total abstinence." Others say it's a punitive approach, demanding forced abstinence—or else.

Antabuse is often combined with other treatments, such as AA. In the Hypnotic Treatment of Alcohol Addiction given in Maudsley Hospital, London, England, hypnotism is combined with Antabuse. Under hypnosis, the patient is told that he will not be able to tolerate even the smell of alcohol without becoming very sick. Antabuse is then given as a safety measure. This is one highly potent form of aversion therapy.

In the use of disulfiram, tranquilizers, and placebos, researchers found in a survey of 103 state hospitals that the rate of improvement a year after treatment was 33%—and varied little no matter what the treatment program. With the use of disulfiram and Temposil, the medication is usually not prescribed without a patient's express desire to submit to this treatment. In fact, prior to receiving this prescription, the patient has to sign a form indicating that the action of the drug has been explained to him.

Personally, I can't think of a more masochistic set-up than taking Antabuse, if there is any chance the person may drink. (And, of course, there always is that chance, if we are talking about a chronic overdrinker.) There certainly is a highly punitive element or the threat of it. Someone once observed that some drinkers drink for the punishment of the hangover, which is self-punishment. This Antabuse-alcohol reaction is that in the extreme. Of the several persons I've known who have taken Antabuse, all of them at one time or another drank while taking it. One "forgot" he'd taken the pill; another said he "didn't give a damn." One nearly died. But this, in no way, affected his drinking behavior thereafter. Clearly it only "works" with certain kinds of people.

According to Dr. Frederick Baekland and Lawrence Lundwall: "Despite the impression of many clinicians that alcoholic persons may benefit from the use of psychotropic medication, most double-blind studies of antidepressants and tranquilizers in alcoholic outpatients have failed to confirm this, either with respect to anxiety and depression or to drinking behavior."

In a booklet put out by the NIAAA it is stated: "Medical research has found no evidence that moderate drinking, even over many years, is in any way hazardous to health. In many ways, an occasional drink is much less harmful to health than the large amounts of unprescribed pills used regularly by Americans for a variety of reasons."

chapter 11

The Nutritional Approach

Why is it that the most intelligent people are often the most stupid about their own body needs? There is the learned professor who can tell you minute details about the Peloponesian Wars, but who doesn't know the difference between a protein and a carbohydrate. Good nutrition is important for everyone—but especially for the drinker. Dr. Roger Williams, one of the discoverer's of the B vitamin family, has stated unequivocally that: "No one who practices the principles of good nutrition will ever become an alcoholic."

According to The National Council on Alcoholism, alcoholics have only one thing in common, the fact that their daily intake of the drug alcohol exceeds their body's ability to handle it effectively. They say, all of us who drink socially, even if we are quite moderate, could be prone to alcoholism, if we don't "watch it." One of the best ways to "watch it" is to pay attention to your body's needs, especially if you have abused your body in the past with excessive use of alcoholic spirits.

Dr. Williams says: "During the years when alcoholism is slowly creeping up on an individual—and everyone agrees that usually years are required—he or she is constantly violating the rules of good nutrition. Obeying these rules will prevent alcoholism from appearing. It is as simple as that."

Most people know enough not to eat several candy bars before dinner. But they might take those same empty calories in the form of an alcoholic drink. The body has a basic capacity for burning a certain amount of fuel, which if furnished in the form of candy or alcohol will eventually crowd out nutritious food. Dr. Williams says: "The joker in this situation is, however, that some individuals (Winston Churchill's an example) can abuse the laws of good nutrition and thrive. If everyone had a body chemistry like that of Winston Churchill, there would be no alcoholism."

It has been estimated that, not infrequently, adult people in our present affluent civilization take one half of their calories each day in the form of alcohol. This, and the assimilation of tons of junk food and white sugar products, has led nutritionists to say we are the most overfed and undernourished people in the world. What is needed is more education in the basic principles of good nutrition, beginning in the elementary schools. Studies have shown that children raised on the empty calories and the quick-energy lift of soft drinks find it very easy to switch to the same empty calories and fast energy boost of alcohol when they grow up.

Each day our bodies need fuel and nutrients such as minerals, vitamins, and amino acids in suitable amounts. If any one of the ingredients is missing, it can cause trouble in the body and brain. As Dr. A. Hoffer, president of the Huxley Institute for Biochemical Research says: "We know that too little protein and too much refined carbohydrates (alcohol, sugar, white flour) are behind the illness and misery suffered by millions of people. We know that people are biochemically different and that some will require many times the recommended daily doses of vitamins and minerals. All this is the subject matter of orthomolecular medicine." He believes that the 1930-1940 period brought us vitamins; the next decade, antibiotics; the 1950s introduced wonder drugs like cortisone; and the 1960s gave us antidepressants and tranquilizers. The 1970s will go down in medical history as the beginning of the orthomolecular era, with its emphasis on biochemical individuality and megavitamin therapy.

We hear a lot today about the amazing successes of megavitamin therapy in treating such illnesses as schizophrenia, neurosis, hypoglycemia, arthritis, senility, and alcoholism. One thing, however, must be made perfectly clear. Megavitamin therapy is not intended to cure a vitamin deficiency (smaller amounts of vitamins would be given for that), but to correct a biochemical imbalance. The physician using megavitamin therapy knows that the illness he treats is not a vitamin deficiency.

The vitamins are given in much larger doses (hence the *mega* prefix meaning "big"). In this therapy, the vitamins are used to correct the balance of faulty body chemistry. (These should be given under the direction of a nutritionally trained physician.) Dr. Williams says: "What is not commonly appreciated is that each one of us has a highly distinctive, individual metabolic personality, an internal biochemistry of his own."

A recovery rate of 71% has been achieved in a two-year study of five hundred alcoholics by Dr. Russell F. Smith of Brighton Hospital, Detroit, Michigan, by giving subjects massive doses of vitamin B_3. Some benefits of B_3, or niacin, treatment are that it changes the chemical effect of alcohol on the individual, reduces mood swings, helps overcome alcoholic insomnia, and reduces tolerance and severity of withdrawal symptoms. Says Dr. Smith,

"While we do not claim B_3 as a cure for alcoholism, we are convinced that it is an important adjunct to traditional treatments . . ."

In an experiment reported in *Quarterly Journal of Studies of Alcohol* with laboratory mice on a poor diet with niacin deficiency, both male and female rats, given a choice, turned to alcohol rather than water. With a nutritional diet plus niacin, they rejected alcohol in favor of water. In a University of California study, rats which inhaled only polluted air also preferred alcohol to water. (Another indication that stress and polluted air can drive one to drink.)

Depression is closely associated with alcoholism. It has been characterized as America's number one mental and emotional illness. The hopelessness of this situation is so devastating that every year approximately sixty thousand cases commit suicide. Antidepressant medications are not very effective. Symptoms of depression include: (1) self-neglect, (2) fatigue, (3) insomnia, (4) deep sadness, and (5) little interest in surroundings.

Nutritionally oriented physicians now see these as a nutritional imbalance, which creates a kind of brain cell starvation that can be cured by megavitamin therapy. In experiment after experiment, when people were deficient in the B complex vitamins, depression was always a symptom. Dr. Linus Pauling has stated "Megavitamins have been successful in treating schizophrenics. I believe they're also effective in combating what we call the blues because a person will be in a better mental and physical health."

A deficiency of thiamine (vitamin B_1) can cause mental depression, fatigue, irritability, confusion, forgetfulness, insomnia, nervousness, and a lack of interest in appearance. A deficiency of niacin can cause total mental confusion, hallucinations, and even a total mental breakdown. Even a mild deficiency will lead to depression. Deficiency of Pantothenic Acid, another B complex vitamin, will lead to mental depression, hot temper, and irritability. Vitamin B_6, in deficiency, can create mental depression, tenseness, and nervousness.

In megavitamin therapy, according to Dr. Klenner, doses include vitamin B_1 in amounts of one thousand milligrams each day. With niacinamide, the dose is five thousand milligrams daily, and with niacin, thirty milligrams about thirty minutes after each meal. Vitamin C therapy begins at fifteen thousand milligrams a day. (All this plus a multivitamin mineral tablet, of course.) These are similar to megadoses given alcoholics.

Many drinkers have a mild, chronic, undetected case of beriberi, the disease of vitamin B_1 deficiency; whose symptoms include breathlessness, swelling of the ankles, and many kinds of heart irregularities. The *British Medical Journal* (1964), reported that chronic heavy drinkers with symptoms of beriberi were treated with massive doses of thiamin (vitamin B_1) with excellent results.

An Australian doctor reported the case of a chronic alcoholic male, with brain deterioration and such lack of muscle coordination that he couldn't walk without staggering and support, who was given a nourishing diet and very high doses of B_1 by injection (about five hundred times that given to nonalcoholics), as well as vitamins B_2 and B_3. In three weeks, he was walking normally and ready to leave the hospital "feeling fine."

Pure carbohydrates make very heavy demands on our supplies of the B vitamins which are not readily stored in the body, and like C, must be replenished daily. There is reason to believe that alcohol consumption makes abnormal demands for the B complex and magnesium. Both B and C vitamins are water soluable.

Dr. Frank S. Butler says: "Alcoholism can be controlled with a diet high in protein and rich in vitamins, especially vitamin B." Dr. Butler notes that those who criticize the alcoholic's drinking probably cannot control their own oral desires, which keep them overweight or chain-smoking which is, in some respects, even more dangerous than alcohol. Dr. Butler calls alcohol a form of "calories only," which kills the appetite for more nutritious foods.

According to Ruth Adams and Frank Murray, writing in their book *Megavitamin Therapy*: "Anyone hooked on sugar finds it easy to swing over to another addiction: black coffee, cigarettes, or alcohol: All of them exerting devastating effects on blood sugar levels." They note: "When one reads of the near miraculous treatment of drug addictions with diet and megadoses of vitamins, one wonders why, while our health officials have bewailed our mounting addiction figures and spent astronomical sums of money investigating supposedly every aspect of it, not a single public official has ever connected addiction with a national diet that is deficient in many essential nutrients and overflowing with pure refined sugar ... a substance that does not exist in nature and which never existed in any quantity in private homes until about fifty years ago or so. We are eating an average of about 120 pounds of sugar each year—each of us." They feel it should be banned or, at least, declared a poison. (Megavitamin therapy is being successfully used in the treatment of alcoholism, drug addiction, and mental illness by Dr. David Hawkins and his staff at North Nassau Mental Health Center, Long Island, New York, for anyone interested.)

Dr. Gustave Standig-Lindberg believes that a lack of magnesium may be responsible for the brain damage that occurs in chronic alcoholism. He says that even when delirium tremens are present, there is no damage to the brain tissues if the patient is getting enough magnesium. He believes that the damage can be reversed by aggressive magnesium therapy. Foods high in magnesium are nuts, seeds, and unprocessed whole grains. It is also available from health food stores as a supplement.

A combination of two vitamins and another common food substance can possibly protect human beings against the harmful effects of both smoking and drinking according to a research team at the Veterans Administration Hospital in Coatesville, Pennsylvania. They tentatively report that heavy drinkers and smokers might be able to use these protective factors to prevent side effects of smoking and drinking, such as heart disease.

Vitamin C and thiamine, known as B_1, plus cysteine, a common compound found in most protein foods combine to make the "magic formula." The investigators, including Dr. Leon J. Gonzales, said these compounds may offer "a means of protection against chronic body insult." Said chief researcher Dr. Herbert Sprince: "I don't want to go on record . . . saying that once you've taking some vitamin C and B_1 to drink and smoke all you want, and it isn't going to hurt you . . . I can't do that . . . I can say that this combination offered rats 100% protection against lethal doses of acetaldehyde, the first step in the body's metabolism of alcohol and a substance that has been implicated in heart disease."

Dr. Sprince said the vitamin-cysteine combination saved the lives of laboratory rats otherwise given lethal doses of acetaldehyde, also found in tobacco smoke. The team said that more research is needed, but there was a strong feeling that, though the experiments were done on rats, this may be helpful for human beings. They found any of the three substances in the "magic compound" helpful, offering the rats some protection, but all three together offered life saving protection from the alcohol and tobacco by-products.

Dr. Roger Williams has designed a supplement for alcoholics called Tycopan, a trade name of the Eli Lilly Co., which contains all the necessary vitamins and minerals you should have every day. It can be obtained under the name Nutricol Forte from Vitamin Quota Inc., Fairfield, N.J. 07006. It may also be purchased under the name of G-154 Nutrients, from General Nutrition Corp., 418 Wood St., Pittsburgh, Pennsylvania 15222. It is available from some Walgreen stores and by prescription from your pharmacy.

Chart of Drinker's Daily Vitamin and Mineral Needs

VITAMINS

Vitamin A	20,000 units	Niacinamide	40 mg.
Vitamin D	1,000 units	Panthothenate	40 mg.
Ascorbic Acid	200 mg.	Vitamin B	10 mg.
Thiamin	4 mg.	Vitamin E_{12}	10 mg.
Riboflavin	4 mg.	Inositol	200 mg.
Pyridoxin	6 mg.	Chline	200 mg.

MINERALS

Calcium	300 mg.	Iodine	0.1 mg.
Phosphate	250 mg.	Iron	10 mg.
Magnesium	100 mg.	Manganese	1. mg.
Copper	1.0 mg.	Zinc	5. mg.

If you are unable to get the compound Tycopan or prefer to take the ingredients separately, this will serve the same purpose. For instance, if you get ten thousand units of vitamin A in your one-a-day pill, take another ten thousand units in a cod liver oil capsule. Take these, of course, in additional to eating nutritious meals, emphasizing fresh fruits and not overcooked, fresh vegetables as well as protein sources such as meat, fish, and dairy products.

If you are working on an abstinence regimen or trying to do controlled drinking, it is very important to know what to eat and what not to touch. According to Dr. Williams, alcoholism is a disease of one's appetites: "This excessive appetite for alcohol is the thing," he says, "that good nutrition can prevent." You have to re-educate your taste buds actually to prefer the foods that are good for you. He recommends that drinkers safeguard their health by taking daily: (1) plenty of proteins such as meat, fish, eggs, cheese; (2) some fresh fruits such as oranges, grapefruit, apples; (3) fresh vegetables, especially the yellow and green ones; (4) one tablespoon of unsaturated fat or oil (corn oil is recommended) used in salad dressing; and (5) supplements: essential vitamins and minerals plus two ounces of glutamine, taken before meals.

We frequently hear that alcoholism will result in cirrhosis of the liver. Yet, according to Dr. Richard Shore and John M. Luce, writing in their book, *To Your Health*: "In spite of the close association (of liver cirrhosis and alcohol), however, only 10% of persons known to be alcohol abusers carry the diagnosis chronic liver disease. This has been used to buttress the claim that cirrhosis of the liver is related more to malnutrition than to alcohol ingestion."

The truth is that cirrhosis of the liver is a mysterious disease of multi-causes which occurs in many people who have never taken a drop of alcohol. It seems to result primarily from a protein deficiency. Insanity, too, can be induced by malnutrition. Both Wernicke's syndrome and Korsakoff's psychosis are also found in nonalcoholic people and appear to be a result of chronic malnutrition, for until the synthesis of the B vitamins in the 1940s, their deprivations were wholly irreversible; but now, cases, if promptly treated, recover with little or no permanent damage.

Another very important supplement is glutamine. Dr. Williams has found that there is strong evidence that in alcoholism glucose metabolism in the brain is impaired. Glucose need in the brain is not only continuous and extensive, but absolutely essential. He says: "The brain cannot function without it, any more than your car can run without fuel." The total amount of glucose needed by the brain every day is about one hundred grams.

A natural substitute for glucose is glutamic acid, an amino acid from proteins. Dr. J.B. Trunnel of Houston, Texas, tells of chronic alcoholics who stopped drinking alcohol when glutamine was administered to them daily without their knowledge. (Glutamine is tasteless and water soluble.) Other studies have confirmed its ability to curb any desire for drink.

Dr. Williams believes that the findings that heavy consumption of alcohol impairs the ability of the brain to utilize glucose is in line with the idea that there must be something deranged in the brain and nervous system of the alcohol or the addiction would not exist. We start out in life with about eight billion brain cells and never produce any more. Good nutrition which supplies vitamins, minerals, and amino acids from proteins, works in the direction of keeping the brain cells healthy, so they won't die. Glutamine is a nutrient not a drug. It will help quiet the nerves and promote sleep. (A cheap source of glutamine is Erex Health Products, P.O. Box 278, Bernhardt, Mississippi 63012. Cost is $2.00 for an ounce or about 14 cents a day. It can be added to water, soups, or milk, or mixed in sauces.)

As important as knowing what to take into your body is knowing what to avoid like the plague. Dr. Harold Rosenbaum, noted nutritionist, has compiled a list of the ten most terrible foods which includes: white bread, fatty bacon, hot dogs, all white sugar products, baby foods, canned sodas, potato chips, French fries, and pickles. He says, "Eat any at your own risk: they are all poisonous."

For super energy, Naura Hayden in her book, *Everything You've Always Wanted to Know About Energy But Were Too Weak to Ask*, recommends taking twice a day: twenty thousand units of vitamin A, two thousand mgs. vitamin C, eight hundred units of vitamin D, four hundred units of vitamin E, plus Dolmite (calcium and magnesium). This is in addition to her "Dynamite Milkshake" which includes: two cups skimmed milk, one tablespoon safflower oil, two packets of sugar substitute, four tablespoons powdered yeast, and four heaping tablespoons lecithin. See her book for instructions on how to make this energy-giving cocktail. Here is another energy booster especially for the overdrinker, contributed by a Drinkwatcher.

> *Hi-vitality Cocktail*
> 1 can frozen orange juice (or skimmed milk)
> ½ tsp. glutamine
> 1 tsp. soy or safflower oil
> 1 tsp. bone meal
> ½ tsp. Brewers yeast
> 1 tsp. honey
> 1 tsp. powdered calcium
> ½ tsp. wheat germ oil

Blend all ingredients in a blender and consume to your good health. Drink one every day, and you'll be on the road to becoming a super man or woman.

Unless you have medical contraindications, there is no reason to give up alcoholic beverages if you drink in moderation, and there may be some benefits to it. In a study done by the Social Research Group of the University of California's School of Public Health, it was found that moderate drinkers outlast both teetotalers and heavy drinkers in length of life. The findings presented to Congress emerged from an analysis of data gathered on 6,159 individuals in four studies done by the group. The results showed substantial increases in early death among frequent heavy drinkers and those judged to have a high number of current problems such as losing a job, troubles with spouse, family, police, etc.

Researcher Robin Room said it was "a curiously persistent finding, one which up to this time defies explanation." It didn't seem to matter what the beverage was, for findings were the same for beer, wine, and hard liquor. The study showed no real cutoff point as to what was the desirable amount to drink. He said: "Our data on general mortality suggests that for the amount of drinking, apparently unlike the amount of smoking, there may be some kind of threshold below which general mortality is little affected."

In the absence of further evidence, he believes, we might as well reinstate "Antsie's Limit" as a sensible suggestion about how to drink without substantially increasing 'the risk of early death. "Antsie's Limit," proposed in 1864 and accepted as safe throughout the 19th century, was: "the equivalent of one and one half ounces of absolute alcohol per day, or about three ounces of whiskey, half a bottle of claret; four glasses of beer, being understood that this is to be taken only at lunch or dinner and that the whiskey is to be well diluted." Alcoholic beverages were used medicinally in our early history.

Ethanol is unique in some aspects of its chemistry. For one thing, it is a very small molecule with infinite water solubility. It can be absorbed by passive diffusion along the entire gastrointestinal tract. It requires no digestion. It is immediately ready to act as a body fuel. When swallowed, it causes a warm sensation as it increases blood flow to the stomach. It heightens the secretion of gastric acid through an excitation of nerve endings in the stomach. The increase in gastric acid secretion, in turn, prompts a rise in the production of digestive enzymes within the pancreas. With most people, 20% to 30% of ethanol is absorbed by the stomach. The rest is mixed with gastric acid and secreted by the stomach. The drug then enters the small intestine.

Alcohol is higher in calories than sugars and starches, although lower in fats. An ounce of liquor contains about seventy calories, about the equal of a chicken drumstick. A twelve-ounce can of beer contains about 150 calories. The calories in alcohol can contribute to overweight, especially as some drinkers tend to eat heavily either before or after drinking as a way to prevent or rid themselves of hangovers. If alcohol is substituted for a balanced diet, the person may lose weight but will surely end up suffering from malnutrition.

The body burns up alcohol through a process of oxidation, which takes place mostly in the liver. You need about one hour to burn up one-half ounce of alcohol. This is the amount contained in an average highball, one glass of wine, or a can of beer. Liquors are distilled beverages: rum, gin, vodka, brandy, and whiskey. They usually contain between 40% and 50% pure alcohol. In this country, liquor is labeled by its proof, which is roughly double its alcoholic content (90 proof means 45% alcohol).

Moderate amounts of alcohol may indeed be less harmful than the "ten most terrible foods," if not actually therapeutic.

Dr. Salvatore Lucia, a highly regarded medical scientist, has recently published his second book on wine as medicine called *A History of Wine As Therapy* (Lippincott), which tells how certain wines produce nutritive, cardiovascular, appetite-arousing, stomachic, diuretic and antibacterial effects. It also describes how wine serves the deep psychological need of mankind for relief from tension and stress.

While for some four thousand years he notes, physicans have known wine could be effective as medicine, it has only been in the last twenty or so years that scientists have understood some of the whys and hows of it. There is already clear evidence that specific wines are useful as therapeutic aids in uncomplicated cases of diabetes; in simple anemias; in such digestive disturbances as the malabsorption syndrome; in the initial treatment of alcoholic cirrhosis; in minimizing acidosis in certain kidney conditions; in the treatment of anorexia; in relieving the infirmities and suffering which accompany old age, and in combating many of the diseases in which anxiety and tension are underlying factors.

"These findings have already led to new and unexpected applications in the prevention and treatment of disease," says Dr. Lucia. He blames the prohibition movement for science not having discovered the whys and hows of wine as medicine generations ago. It scared investigative scientists, he says, with demon-alcohol propaganda: "Since the beginning of history, man has doused himself with wine as medicine. Whole schools of medicine were based upon wine. As early as the second century after Christ, the great physician Galen was classifying wines by types and recommending them for specific physiological effects." Dr. Lucia is pleased to note it is not the alcohol in the wine that performs the healing, but other ingredients not all of which are as yet identified.

Other benefits of moderate drinking mentioned by researchers are increased gains in self-confidence and ability to relax; a decrease in the "jitters"; aid in performing difficult or odious tasks; the promotion of a general feeling of well being, optimism, and increased "masculineness." It also helps one to have fun and laugh more, it is a tranquilizer, and it takes the edge off an intolerable reality. However, with increased amounts of liquor, the gains often deteriorate into losses, such as nervousness turning into acute anxiety; less social ease and interaction; more difficulty coping; depression; more negative self-concept, and more regressive, childish behavior.

Dr. Salvatore P. Lucia, professor of medicine at the University of California Medical School, discussed in an address to Vanderbilt University Medical School "the joys of wine and its concealed healing powers," observing that iron in table wines may aid in com-

bating iron deficiencies in anemia and the wine itself may control
obesity, saying that the tranquilizing effect can lessen the anxiety
which often causes a person to overeat. He said, "Wine, in small
quantities, increases salivation, gently stimulates gastric activity,
and aids in normal evacuation. Because of its antibacterial action,
wine has been recommended in the treatment of intestinal colic,
colitis, constipation, diarrhea, and various infections of the gastrointestinal tract."

Dry wines (those low in sugar) are often used in the diet of
diabetics. Dr. Henry dolger, director of the diabetes clinic at
Mount Sinai Medical Center, said: "I don't frown on the moderate
use of alcohol for my patients . . . Most of my patients drink socially . . . Diabetes is not, in itself, incompatible with drinking."

The Vodka Information Service of New York once issued a
statement that physicians still prescribe distilled spirits as heart
medicine. Vodka is a colorless unaged liquor of neutral spirits that
is considered the most impurity free of all alcoholic beverages, having the least amount of congeners which can contribute to toxic
reactions. It is well to remember, with distilled spirits, the darker
the drink, the more congeners.

There is a German saying: "Your brewery is your best
medicine." In a recent study published in the *New England Journal
of Medicine*, of 7,705 healthy men living in Honolulu, who were
then examined six years later, the findings were that drinking beer
or liquor can cut chances of heart attack in half. Dr. George
Rhoads said: "the more they drank—up to three or four beers a
day—the fewer of them got heart disease." Said Dr. Abraham
Kagan, director of the study: "If you are a moderate drinker and
drink approximately three beers a day or about two shots of liquor,
it could well stop you from having a heart attack." The Honolulu
researchers believe that there may be a link between use of alcohol
and production within the body of alpha cholesterol—a beneficial
form of cholesterol.

Used with prudence, wine and spirits can add pleasure and
health to life. Wine is an excellent tranquilizer. As Dr. Russell V.
Lee says: "There is no doubt at all that moderate use of wine while
eating is the pleasantest and probably the most effective tranquilizer known to medical men." It is a much pleasanter and more
relaxing experience, as he points out, than popping a hastily swallowed pill. (And probably much better for you, being less toxic.) So
if you watch your nutritional needs, there is no reason you can't enjoy an occasional glass of wine. But don't abuse, lightly use.

chapter 12

Alcoholism: A Family Affair?

Alcoholism, along with drug addiction and criminality, is often viewed as a failure of the family system. The family may have been pulled apart or been unable to function well due to many causes: deaths, divorces, poverty, too many siblings, vocational demands, illnesses, or just sheer distances. And many alcoholics have no families at all or, at least none they feel that can turn to for help or comfort; and thus they turn to the extended family of a social club or the community at large for a sense of belonging and guidance. (Let us never forget that we, the ones with families somewhat intact, are the lucky ones, and try to appreciate this blessing.)

One real problem for many alcoholics, as for many of the rest of us, is trouble within a marriage. Intense marital conflict, separation, and divorce are strikingly present among alcoholic persons. And it would be hard to say which came first, the marriage problem or the drinking problem. Some say, emphatically, it was the disintegration of the marriage that caused the excessive drinking. Others say just the reverse. Marital status does seem to offer, at least, a clue to life adjustment in which it is expected that the less well-adjusted group would have a higher proportion of heavy drinkers than those currently married.

Often the wives of alcoholic men have been characterized as "bitches" who drive fine men to drink. These wives are described as castrating women, who hold their husbands by over-mothering them and keeping them psychological babies. One psychiatrist found that his patient needed to be married to an alcoholic and became threatened by any signs of her husband sobering up. Another researcher found that wives of alcoholics were no more disturbed than wives of nondrinking mates. Yet there persists a picture of the long-suffering wife whose friends and family encourage to leave her alcoholic spouse and seek support and redress in the law courts. The marriage generally cannot be saved then, for as John Barrymore once observed: "Love cannot be saved once the point of litigation has been reached; for the same reason that paper handkerchiefs never return from the laundry."

Researchers have identified five specific behavior patterns of typical wives of drinking mates in the early stages: (1) attempts to safeguard family interests, (2) withdraws from the marriage, (3) attacks mate, (4) acting out and (5) tries to protect husband from outside world. In this particular study, 70% of the wives married the husbands before the onset of heavy drinking. A study shows that alcoholic women tend to marry alcoholic husbands, especially the second time around. The husbands also tend to respond in counterproductive ways to the wife's drinking, similar to that cf the wives of drinking mates.

Often both partners in a marriage drink too much. What then? One might think that this would work out, as they've both got the same problem and could be understanding. However, the mere presence of the partner may serve as a drinking cue. Both may not want to drink at the same time. Actually, it doesn't work out unless both are willing to add some form and discipline to their lives. they both must find new and positive ways of interacting together that reinforces positive, life-enhancing behavior.

In an experiment that took place at George Washington University in 1975, the spouses of alcoholics joined their partners in the hospital for treatment. Assistant Professor of Psychiatry, Peter Steinglass referred to the program as "a fascinating venture . . . for both treaters and treated." Not only did the program not ban alcohol, booze was openly served to the couples. The idea was to simulate, as much as possible, the home situation during the ten-day observation in the hospital. Efforts were made to make the hospital environment as "homey" as possible. Alcohol was freely available for the first seven days. As the couple went about the usual business of living, shopping, preparing their own meals, participating in therapy and recreational activities, the therapists were able to gain insight into the prevailing "family dynamics," focusing especially on what might precipitate a bout of excessive drinking.

"The program not only does not insist on the usual abstinence model of treatment, but actually suggests that intoxicated behavior can be utilized by the therapist as an adjunct to treatment . . . Instead of viewing the individual alcohol abuser as the problem, therapy is directed at the couple as a whole unit," said Dr. Steinglass in a interview.

The program has three phases: an initial two-week prehospital phase of three sessions per week of counseling; the ten-day in-patient phase of counsel; and then follow up. Despite the briefness of the hospital stay, therapists were very effective in being able to identify repetitive and predictable drinking patterns by the third or fourth day of hospitalization. They were able to gain a clear-cut understanding of the relationship between drinking behavior and the couples' interactional life in a very short time.

"We would suggest," said Steinglass, "that the hospitalization of a couple or an entire family, with open access to alcohol in the therapeutic situation may provide valuable information that will give momentum to change in a previously intractable drinking situation." While admitting that the program was highly experimental, Dr. Steinglass wished to avoid generalizing about the impact of the program on couples not highly motivated to change or those in which the marriages were just too unstable. The program has most success with middle class, intact couples, who display a substantial degree of economic and interactional stability.

One specific case involved a husband and a wife who had a bad drinking problem. The husband would return from work in the late afternoon to find his wife "in her cups" and highly intoxicated. She would be tearful, depressed, and sometimes suicidal. The therapist and other couples in the gorup noted that it was only when the wife was intoxicated that the husband showed any real affection for her and that these "bouts with the bottle" often ended in the couple's making love. When the therapist pointed this out to the couple, the husband began to avoid overinvolvement with his wife when she was intoxicated and the wife began to work at being more loving and affectionate with her husband when she was sober. The association of the excessive use of alcohol and sex had to be broken. Gradually, the marriage became better and the drinking non excessive.

While the patients in this experiment were only required to attend one daily ninety-minute couples group therapy session they tended to involve themselves most enthusiastically in marathon therapy sessions and interacted with each other in spirited talks about their problems and possible solutions. In the evenings, they could view videotapes of the therapy sessions. Dr. Steinglass said, "After only the first week in the hospital, there was often renewed optimism about the marital relationship and the sense of joy that comes from taking positive action toward altering your life. One couple celebrated their twenty-fifth anniversary on the ward and requested reservations for the fiftieth."

A facility called The Meadows, of Wickenburg, Arizona, has begun offering a three-day treatment program for families of alcohol abusers, believing that maladaptive behavior patterns first develop in the family and sometimes these patterns go unrecognized by the families themselves. The program is to help the families recognize the problems and point out ways in which they can reorganize their own lives, irrespective of what the addictive person does.

The program is aimed not only at providing methods of self-help for the "significant others" in the chemically dependent person's life, but also at assuring a more conducive home life for such a person after treatment. In many cases the alcoholic's employer urges family members to attend the family program sessions, stressing that there has been an increase in broken homes as a result of treating chemically dependent persons without treating the "significant others" for their problems.

Vicki Gannon, family program director, says that family members are often fearful that the recovering alcoholic will outgrow them in personal development. Treatment of family groups begins with an overview of chemical dependency, emphasizing the family dynamics that lead to the dysfunction. Through group therapy, with support from their peers, individuals discover the attitudes which have been causing problems. They then make a commitment to work on changing those attitudes when they return home. (For further information, contact David J. Brick, Director, The Meadows, P.O. Box 97, Wickenburg, Arizona 85358).

Thus cojoint, or family therapy, is achieving great popularity today, based on the core belief that couples and families function symbiotically or "feed off each other." The behavior of the one part affects all parts or the whole. Excessive drinking, then, is not seen as one individual expressing deviant behavior, but as a symptom of a malfunctioning family system. The treatment, thus, must involve treating the whole family unit. In a marriage, drinking of one person could serve the unconscious needs of the spouse, or of both partners, as evidence of unequal power distribution or as a scapegoat for aggression. Thus, the alcoholic is seen as no sicker than the other mate; rather, it is believed the whole family unit is disturbed and in distress.

The Palm Beach Institute of West Palm Beach, Florida, has a completely family-oriented approach to helping alcoholics. This lovely Gold Coast facility is often called a "last resort"—as the cure often works when all others have failed. Basking in the Florida sun, the facility has six small buildings in a charming residential section of Florida. Patients range in age from teens to old-timers. (A cure here, however, is not cheap at $395 a week.) One of the Institute's most visible and publicized successes was Rep. Wilbur Mills, who signed in after press coverage of his misadventures with a stripper and when other rehabilitation techniques had failed. After two months at the Institute (and a $3,950 fee), he returned from the Institute to his seat in the House, hopefully cured of his drinking problem.

The Institute's basic theme is that a person's alcoholism is indicative of a breakdown in his family. Treatment is a combination of group therapy, individual counseling, lectures, psychodrama, and self-analysis. This generally lasts about eight weeks. In the last two months of treatment, at least one of the patient's family members enters the institute for two weeks, as, indeed, did Mrs. Mills. The Institute's director, Dr. Ronald J. Catanzaro, a psychiatrist, says: "The treatment of the family is part of the core of the patient's problem. It's the whole family's problem because it shows a poorly functioning family." He says about six out of ten who take the cure there stay off alcohol.

Dr. Cantanzaro's interest in alcoholism developed because of his own mother's drinking problem. He developed the family treatment technique borrowing heavily from many other sources and disciplines. On his staff are psychologists and social workers, specially trained, and several former alcoholics. Upon admittance, each patient is assigned a counselor who will guide him through each phase of treatment. The days will be tightly structured with no time to be depressed.

Patients carry notebooks in which are progress reports and a self-help journal to be used between sessions. They may also write "fantasy letters" to people who have annoyed or are bothering them, which are discussed, but not mailed. No unauthorized medication is permitted, although some drugs may be prescribed for those who arrive in bad shape and need sleep or are afraid of seizures. Dr. Cantanzaro says: "It gets to be a kind of life and death sort of thing when patients are made to realize that their behavior is making it unlikely they are going to survive very long and they see how they've been managing their lives and families—then they get a real urgency to get well."

Al-Anon is a group of relatives of alcoholics who band together to help each other with their common problems. It helps many women to either break away from the alcoholic partner or to desensitize herself from him emotionally so that she can function better and won't continue any game playing with the alcoholic. Women have been helped in Al-Anón, even though the mate refused to stop drinking or get any help for the problem.

Al-Anon has suggestions for the spouse of an alcoholic which includes: live one day at a time, don't get impatient (the problem didn't develop overnight); accept the fact you must change; discuss serious matters only when your mate is sober; be abstinent in your own habits; don't hide or throw out bottles of booze; don't nag or preach or open old wounds. They further suggest: don't make threats you are not prepared to carry out; don't lose your temper; don't make excuses for the alcoholic, and don't call in for him to work saying he's sick. Don't lose your temper and don't seek revenge; and finally, don't use the appeal: "If you really loved me . . .". The sum of their message is, the only person you can really change is yourself. As an alternate to Al-Anon (or in addition to it), you might discuss your problem with a psychiatrist, social worker, minister, or counselor; or consider some other form of group therapy.

If you really love your mate, I see no reason you should divorce him (or her) just because he drinks. He can be helped to become abstinent or even, possibly, to learn to moderate his habits. It is interesting to note that in certain Indian settlements, the families do not reject the drinking member. In many groups, it is reported that families and communities excuse the overdrinker for his drunken sprees and some observers explicitly deny that in these settlements heavy drinking leads to broken marriages or loss of family. Because they are not rejected and displaced, reports have shown that the Indian drinkers feel less guilt and self-pity in regard to their drinking. And in many cases, reportedly, they are able to either to give up alcohol or learn to moderate their drinking to a sensible degree.

chapter 13

Women and Alcohol:

Special Problems

Today we hear a lot about how the secret drinking of women is no secret any more. In an interview, Dr. Morris Chafetz said, "When I first came into the field more than twenty-two years ago, the statistics showed 5½ male alcoholics to one female. The present figures show a ratio of about three to one—that is an 83% increase in the ratio of problem drinkers who are women." Dr. Don Cahalon and other authorities say the ratio is now up to one to one.

Chafetz believes this rise is due to the changing role of women in American society, as "one of the rites of passage in our society is drinking." Also it is thought to be due to the social milieu of bars which is now a mixed company of both men and women. Chafetz believes women drink more in the company of other women than around men. He says, "I think so, since biologically and socially we prefer to be on our best behavior with the opposite sex. To put it simply, you never get a lover being sloppy."

He believes that women who drink alcoholically are depressed, live a lot in isolation, are lonely, with either physical, psychological, or social pain. He says, "Remember, alcohol is an anesthetic drug—it makes you feel less hurt." He believes women problem drinkers are harder to spot than men because of their many protective devices. "For one, fewer of them work, so they drink in the home, where you can't recognize it as readily." For years, he says, there has been a male chauvinistic attitude toward alcoholism claiming it as a male disease. "We built up a system not to notice a woman with a drinking problem. She was a double stigma—she was both unladylike and she was pretty lousy to act that way. We crippled women with a kind of veneration. It's all part of putting a woman down by putting her up. People looked the other way until she was finally so obviously a serious alcoholic, that she was down-the-road by the time she came in for treatment."

This double stigma is not only prevalent in this country, but abroad as well. In the Soviet Union, alcoholism seems to be largely a masculine problem because strong stigma still attaches to the admitted female alcoholic. Women are rarely seen drunk in public, but with men, it is all too noticeable! Both women and men drinkers, incidentally, had better watch out in Russia, for to be caught drinking and driving is no joke in Moscow. The first time the driver's license is suspended one year; the second time, for three years; the third time, forever.

Dr. P.C. Whitehead of Canada has said that in 1970, women accounted for one in every five cases of alcohol poisoning. Today, there is one case among women for every two cases among men in his country. He, too, believes that the changing roles of women in modern society may be a cause. Although recent studies show an alarming growth rate in feminine alcoholism, it has occurred before. In the last century every house in London sold gin, which became known as "mother's ruin." (One study stated that alcoholic women tended to have rigid, domineering mothers.)

It may be that alcoholism is one of the prices that women are paying for their increased economic emancipation. Women do pay more dearly for alcohol abuse than men. In some areas still, according to society, a woman who drinks heavily is thought to have "abandoned her femininity"; even though, traditionally, alcohol has always been used by many women, especially during painful menstrual periods, as a means of self-medication.

In a study at the University of Oklahoma, it was found that women taking oral contraceptives metabolize alcohol more slowly than women not on the pill. The slower alcohol metabolism in women taking the pill, they say, may be caused by the action of estrogen or other hormones in the birth control drug. These findings were reported by Dr. Ben Morgan Jones, at the annual meeting of the Mexican Society of Nutrition and Endocrinology, at Acapulco, Mexico.

Richard Zylman, of the Center for Alcohol Studies at Rutgers, did a study of male and female drunk drivers. Instead of the usual figure given of 50% to 85% percent of fatal accidents being caused by drunk drivers, he estimates the figure at 43%, which is still high. Apparently the role of the drunk driver is relatively minor in ordinary crashes, but it is high with the fatal ones. Safety researcher

W.L. Carlson attributes it to "inexperience with drinking and driving." With men, the peak age for alcohol-involved, fatal crashes is twenty-one, which is around the age that most young men are just starting to use alcohol.

Women, apparently, don't have these "danger years," as compared with males. There are much fewer female drunks on the road than men. When a women driver does drink, however, she is more likely than the male to have a crash, even at a relatively lower blood alcohol concentration. Carlson regards this, too, as a manifestation of inexperience with drinking and driving. It is an interesting point, since a woman's body is made up of only 55%-65% water, as opposed to 65%-75% for a man. Women need less liquor to reach the same BAC (blood/alcohol/concentration) as a man.

Dr. W. Feurlein of Germany did a study which showed a sociological difference between male and female alcoholics. The female alcoholics, he found, were significantly much more likely to come from the upper levels of society; the males, much more likely to come from the lower classes. In an American study of drinkers, women college graduates were found to be much more likely to drink than other women but, if they drank, they were also much less likely to be heavy drinkers than drinkers who never finished high school.

There seems to be a correlation between self-assertion, independence, intelligence, and drinking among women. Among the Makua, who live in Tanzania in Africa, family ties are loose and, in general, the women have more power of decision than the men. The Makua women drink a lot and are not criticized for it by other tribe members. (Alcohol in Tanzania means a local brew called palm wine and beer.) In other words, women in the power position do what they like. (This has probably always been the case.)

Dr. Joan Curlee, a clinical psychologist at the Menninger Clinic, Topeka, Kansas, studied one hundred women suffering from alcoholism and found that twenty-one of them suffered from the "empty-nest" syndrome. This study concluded that one in five women was driven to drink because she felt her family no longer needed her. Dr. Curlee said: "For twenty-one of these women, the situation that triggered the alcoholism was in some ways related to changes in their roles as wives and mothers. They had all been reasonably stable until then, and they had showed no previous indication to themselves or others that drinking might be a problem."

These women were all middle-aged and they had all apparently been unusually dependent on their husbands and children for a sense of both identify and self-worth. Some of them were widows or divorcees—and had feelings of emptiness and loneliness. They felt unloved and hopeless and said: "Life lacks meaning."

Dr. Curlee said: "All of them, as soon as they began to drink heavily, began to retreat into the solitude of their homes. They took up secret drinking, which has been described as the most typical drinking pattern among American women alcoholics."

In another US survey, men abstainers put higher emphasis on doing so for financial or vocational reasons. Women placed more emphasis on the social, religious, or moral reasons for abstention. It was also found that women drinkers are much more likely to become social isolates, with a narrow range of friends than heavy drinking males who will gravitate to the social ties of drinking with men at work, at bars, or in the local taverns.

While the double standard is certainly on the way out in most urban areas, public opinion is still much harder on a women who drinks than a man. The different attitudes can be observed in the stock phrases we hear like: "She drove him to drink" (or as they would say in more sophisticated circles: "She has an unconscious investment in keeping him drunk." Of the man who lives with an alcoholic women, comments are typically: "He's a jerk to put up with it." Women's Lib is trying to change the image of the woman who drinks. ("If you do a man's job, you should be able to drink like a man.") But old ideas die slowly . . . you still hear a woman who drinks being called a lush or other denigrating terms. However, the trend indicates that no name-calling is now going to stop women from drinking and assuming some other formerly all male prerogatives.

A German group did a study of addiction and suicide, which found that men are less prone to suicide than women, and housewives more than women with other occupations. The report said suicide attempts come to a peak between the ages of seventeen and thirty-five years of age. It revealed that 75% of the suicide attempts were made under the influence of some drugs or alcohol. (The preferred method was the use of sleeping pills.)

The study showed that suicide was twenty-two times greater among addicts than the general public in the same age group. Almost 40% of the addicts in the sample had attempted suicide at least once. (The report was made of patients transported by ambulances to hospitals.) According to the researchers, the situations most likely to lead to suicide are a reaction to the loss of a loved partner, isolation, loneliness, fears, and a feeling of helplessness. (All these things, so frequently, are the lot of abandoned women.)

Some experts have said that alcoholism is an attempt at a self-cure of an untenable inner conflict, which might be called "suicide by ounces." In the past, most women built their lives around a man and if anything happened to that relationship, they were wiped out emotionally and often financially. Many of these women turned to alcohol for solace. They did not have a career interest to make their life worthwhile. They were too frightened and reclusive to attempt to find another mate. Fearing rejection, immorality, and promiscuity, they came to reject the opposite sex as a source of satisfaction and turn to an object, a thing, the bottle, as being more dependable in gratification and less threatening. So many women take to drink as a reaction to the disappointment of a love affair or marriage that ends badly and/or sadly.

A relatively new group especially for women is *Women For Sobriety*, founded in 1975 by sociologist Jean Kirkpatrick. The organization is based on the philosophy that a person starts drinking to cope with loneliness, frustration, emotional deprivation, or other stresses. "The great barrier to a woman alcoholic's recovery is her lack of self-esteem," says Dr. Kirkpatrick. She points out that nine out of ten alcoholic women are abandoned by their husbands, while only one out of ten male alcoholics is deserted by his wife. She believes women who are alone are especially vulnerable to alcoholism. The group is abstinence-oriented and has a thirteen-step acceptance program. (Dr. Kirkpatrick can be reached at 344 Franklin Street, Quakertown, Pa. 18951.)

In a study by Dr. Don Cahalan, the findings indicated that for men, environmental factors do play a more conspicuous role in problem drinking while for women, alienation, survival-anxiety, and maladjustment were the key factors. Women with drinking problems tended to score higher in psychological maladjustment than did men with the same problem. Surprisingly, in this study, fully one third of both men and women reported that they had drinking problems at a certain point in their lives, but were either problem-free three years later or were able to greatly decrease their alcohol intake for a variety of reasons, such as health, finances, or increased maturity. Thus, it is possible to drink alcoholically at one time and later "mature out" of the destructive behavior, either spontaneously, through therapy, or with a little help from a kind fate.

chapter 14

Teens and Alcohol:

New Trends

According to Dr. Ernest Noble: "We have a potential problem drinking population of over 7 million teenagers." He believes that TV commercials reinforce the myth that alcohol consumption marks the "rite of passage from adolescence to adulthood." He cites one commercial that shows a bartender asking a teenager for proof of his legal drinking age. After checking the ID, the bartender grins, wishes the kid a "happy birthday" and hands him a frosty glass of beer.

Dr. Noble objects to this kind of beer advertising. Senator William Hathaway and Rep. Paul Rogers are said to be thinking about what used to be unthinkable—banning all alcohol ads from TV. (Hard liquor commercials are already outlawed.) Some brewers have canceled their commercials in response to these objections. But the industry, in general, spends $500 million to promote drinking. And, of course, these ads are seen by teenagers.

Teenage girls, a recent study has shown, are now drinking as much as boys and becoming intoxicated as often, in certain areas of the US. Researchers Dr. Henry Wechsler and Mary McFadden, of the Medical Foundation of Boston, reported their findings to the Rutger's *Journal of Studies on Alcohol*. Only ten years ago, girls in the teen bracket were far behind boys in drinking behavior. The report affirmed that the margin of difference between the proportion of both sexes who drink is rapidly decreasing.

Make no mistake about it, however, alcohol in excessive amounts can kill. In 1974, in South Boston, a sixteen-year-old boy died after drinking a pint of vodka without pausing. He drank it apparently on a bet. In Fort Walton, Florida, two men in their thirties died after each consumed more than a quart of gin, trying to settle a bet over who could hold the most liquor.

When teens switched from drugs to alcohol, many parents applauded because, after all, alcohol is a legal substance and most drugs are illegal. But now teen drinking is becoming a real problem. To some experts, the problem of teens and alcohol has been there all along . . . the drug scare just distracted everyone's attention. Lowered drinking ages have made alcoholic beverages much more available to teens.

According to a study by Yankelovitch, Skelly, and White, however, though many of the students do use alcohol and drugs, few are really abusers. Yankelovitch found that: "Young people do not try drugs instead of alcohol, but in addition to it. Alcohol, in fact, continues to be used far more generally than drugs. We found twice as many drinkers as drug abusers (58% in high school, 79% in college). Most students, regardless of age, believe that alcohol is more dangerous than pot but that doesn't keep them from drinking." (These findings were also revealed in a recent poll of teens by Scholastic Magazines.)

Another interesting finding was that the personality patterns of drug and alcohol users were strongly similar. These teens were more self-directed and liberal in their views, as compared with non-users. But the important point of the study is that the vast majority of drug users, including alcohol users, are not drug abusers. They do not depend on drugs for psychological reasons. The study said: "They have not dropped out and they are not undermotivated; in fact, their grades are the same as nonusers . . . They use drugs for the same reasons that adult social drinkers use liquor." The conclusions seem to be that only a minor number of high school students are a risk for drug abuse in the future. Yankelovitch said that these were students engaged in "acting out" behavior in various forms; such as damaging property, staying out late and cutting up in school.

A study by The Research Triangle Institute for the National Institute on Alcohol Abuse and Alcoholism, indicated young drinkers most often reported wanting "to have a good time" as their principal reason for using alcohol. Few young people, if any, mentioned drinking as an escape from trouble, personal inadequacies, or other negative reasons. This research data contradicts the widely held view that teens drink to be grown-up. However, the report did indicate that young people tend to follow the drinking practices of their parents. Religion was correlated with a lower drinking rate among youth, although the report said, "the deterrent effect was not strong."

As might be expected, young people who earned high grades in school were less likely to drink; and if they did, they were inclined to be infrequent drinkers. On the other hand, of students making low grades, just as many were abstainers as heavy drinkers. Parental approval or disapproval of drinking has little effect on the males who drink, according to the survey. Girls, however, who report problem drinking patterns more often say their parents disapprove of girls' drinking, while they remain noncommittal about that of boys.

Drs. Shirley and Richard Jessor, who conducted a four-year study of a group of 432 adolescents, focused on a variety of personality, environmental, and behavioral factors which might be related to the onset of drinking. Their main tool was a sixty-page questionnaire administered to the participants.

The research revealed that as young people began to drink they moved toward a pattern of greater independence, placing less value on academic achievement and showing less involvement with religion; expressing greater tolerance of deviancy; becoming more oriented towards their peers and parents, and engaging in more acts of general deviance. Those who never began to drink differed from the drinkers in a number of ways, developing what the researchers called a "pattern of conventionality." These young people placed a higher emphasis on academic achievement and conformance. According to doctors Jessor, youths do see drinking as a symbol of adulthood, and efforts to prevent alcohol misuse might well be aimed at ways to end the perception of drinking as an indicator of growing up.

If you have a teen drinker in your home who might be called an underachiever, Dr. Saul Kapel says you should examine his sense of self-esteem. He might be suffering from what teachers call a developmental lag, from which he'll recover, or an assortment of learning disabilities, or emotional problems that stand in his way. If he (or she) performs consistently below your or his teacher's expectations, he may need special help, such as therapy or counseling. The drinking could be only a symptom . . . Dr. Kapel says that fear of criticism often works the hardest against students. He says a loss of self-esteem can be linked to criticism given in a negative way. "I've long noticed that youngsters from homes in which parents freely criticize one another with respect, dignity, and an occasional touch of humor, usually perform better in school. They get the message at home that one doesn't have to hide his weaknesses and, as a result, they can admit mistakes and handle criticism without loss of pride."

The use of alcohol seems to be tied to the search for independence and, conversely, the fear of dependency on people. William and Joan McCord, in the 1930s, did research on 510 boys which led them to speculate that an alcoholic's early background caused conflicts over dependence and independence and a weak self-image. Those in their study who later became alcoholics tried to resolve this conflict by a facade of independence and aggressive masculinity. As adults, they used alcohol as an outlet which allowed them to be dependent on a drug rather than people—yet they seem independent and masculine.

If you live in a home with a drinking teenager who is getting into alcohol-related trouble, I'd advise consulting an objective third party. This could be a therapist, counselor, or minister. The problem may be situational and pass by itself, but talking over problems may help to prevent further trouble. If your teen won't get help, I'd suggest you get some help for yourself in order to cope with him or her.

It often happens that teens need help because of a drinking parent. Al-Teens is an outgrowth of Al-Anon and it tries to help young people understand their parents' drinking problems and find some support for their own problems in a group setting. Meetings are AA-oriented.

ACCEPT (Alcoholism Center Coordinating Education, Prevention and Treatment) has a special program for young people, ages twelve to twenty, who have a drinking problem. Unlike other organizations which are entirety self-help, ACCEPT is run by professionals—psychiatrists, psychologists, social workers—and the goal of the program is to deal with the underlying problem (anxiety, fear, frustration, etc.) that led to the drinking in the first place. (Further information about their programs can be had from Charles Packham, Community Resource Consultant, ACCEPT, 300 Park Ave., S., New York, N.Y. 10010.)

Behavior therapy can be used at home by parents to rehabilitate substance abusers among adolescents, according to John Cassady at the Social Adjustment Center, 1710 W. Colonial Drive, Orlando, Florida 32804. Mr. Cassady directed a pilot study project, testing this approach on adolescent probationers and said: "It was most effective in five out of eight cases. The basic idea is that teens and parents can work together by the use of contracts negotiated between them in which the children pledge to meet their parents wishes for more appropriate behavior in return for certain rewards.

Parents who had formerly relied solely on punishment as discipline, found that changing parental behavior led to behavior change in their adolescents. At an initial meeting, the Social Adjustment Center's outpatient counseling clinic will determine what rewards will be most effective in each situation and discover what behavior the parents most want changed. Once a week adolescents and parents meet with the counselor to discuss progress. While all teens in the study had severe problems with alcohol and drugs in the beginning, the progress made was heartening. This method may prove useful in many communities for dealing with young drug and alcohol abusers. (It should be noted that teen problems with alcohol show up more in confrontation with authority figures such as police and courts, rather than in health problems such as, liver trouble, etc.)

Here could be a way to overcome the communications gap that so often exists between youth, parents, and other authority figures. Family therapy can be most useful for teens and parents. The family therapists do not attack drinking directly and this reduces blaming and makes the situation easier all around. They try to help teens to solve problems in a more adaptive manner than drinking. Excessive drinking is often associated, both in teens and adults, with alienation from the family. The therapists ask the question: "What do you want to become?"

In a study that compared family behavior patterns of mothers of adolescent drug abusers with a group of mothers who had teens, but no adolescent drug abusers in the family: the Texas Research Institute found that the mothers of abusers were much more "disidentified with their own mothers." They were, also, inclined to describe their teenagers as much more "resentful and bitter" than the control group. (Both groups were matched by age, ethnic background and socioeconomic status.) All the mothers, also, tended to describe the fathers as significantly more "arrogant and critical." The picture they gave was of an unhappy home life.

It is important that our young people understand that manhood is much more than a measure of how much beer and booze they can drink. Fraternities should stop having initiation rites using alcohol like the one of the Siaseli fraternity at Stevens College, which consisted of going to five or six bars and drinking large quantities of alcohol. Last year an initiate needed life support systems to save him, and this year, David Hoffman, 21, died after making the "rounds." Hopefully, campuses across the country will take a stand against this kind of sadistic stupidity—causing so much unnecessary pain and death by alcohol poisoning.

A Baltimore priest, Father Joseph C. Martin, urges a common sense approach to alcohol use both in teens and adults who drink. In a recent interview, after addressing a gathering of the Psychiatric Institute in Washington, D.C., he said: "True drug education is the teaching of values and ideals to youth. Parents should convey to their children ideals strong enough to withstand peer pressure," which he describes as "the most important factor in drinking by youth."

"My message to parents," he says, "is that life is composed of pleasant and unpleasant parts. If you can teach your child to cope with both without chemicals, you've succeeded (as parents)." Father Martin taught high school subjects in preparatory seminaries before his superiors in the Baltimore Archdiocese granted him permission, in 1970, to be a full-time professional in the alcoholism field. By then he had already spent much time lecturing on alcohol abuse after being treated himself, in 1958, at Guest House, a facility for alcoholic priests in Michigan.

While some people in the older generation in every generation offer the implicit and explicit message that the youth of our nation are going to hell, statistics do show that 1.3 million teens and pre-teens are drinking to excess, according to NIAAA. Of these, some four hundred and fifty thousand have been called alcoholics. In a survey, 70% of all high school students either drink or have explored alcohol. Teens are not only drinking more, but at a younger age. Alarmists call it a "national crisis" but calmer voices say it is part of a trend caused by the speedup of electronic communications and TV. Teens are growing up faster in all departments. Fortunately, more help is being offered teens in regard to alcohol education and prevention programs than ever before.

The American Red Cross has recently added an alcohol program for youth to its services, aimed at helping teens fourteen to seventeen years of age. The module consists, basically, of alcohol information to be conducted by teens and adult volunteers for high school and junior high school students in many of the nation's approximately three thousand and two hundred Red Cross chapters. Sessions provide information about alcohol and its effect on the body, discussion of the reasons why people drink, the cultural origins of drinking, and the function of drinking in today's teen society, among other topics. Michael Lenaghan is the Director. (For details, write Youth Service Program, American Red Cross, 17th and D Streets, Washington, D.C. 20006.)

In speaking of young people, Dr. Z. Thielle of Poland, stresses the right of the seeker after solutions to be helped to find his own: "We should lead a man to his truth, reveal to him his needs and his problems. A therapist has no right to impose his own truth, it is ethically wrong and senseless." He believes it is stress factors in contemporary society that push young people into drug and alcohol abuse.

Dr. Ernest Noble, Director of NIAAA, while still conceding alcoholism to be a disease, has said recently he would not pin the label "alcoholic" on drinkers who are not adults: "When dealing with teens especially, the trend today is to drop the label 'alcoholic' and use the term 'problem drinker'." In an interview in the *New York Times*, he stated: "A kid may go through a phase where he uses the stuff. And he may overcome it as he grows older. He may be caught up in a social milieu . . . He may be picked up on a drunken-driving charge; but only once; later there may not be anything like that for him. Let's face it, our society still stigmatizes against the alcoholic, so we try to approach the problem with kids without the silly label 'alcoholic'."

Senator Charles McC. Mathias says society must develop new prevention strategies for youth involving schools, parents, youth workers, government officials, the courts, and young people, themselves, in order to cope with the rising level of disruptive behavior on the part of the nation's youth. He noted that the increase in alcohol and drug offenses in the schools rose more than one third from 1970 to 1973. The search for new ways to control youthful violence and disruptive behavior "is a variation on an old theme—prevention or 'punishment." He noted that traditional punishments, such as suspension and expulsion from school are seldom effective.

Eva Schindler-Raiman, an organizational alcohol consultant, emphasizes that prevention requires a positive approach, one oriented toward the future rather than the present. Teens should be told: "We really can control our future," she commented, "if we are able to engage in realistic dreaming."

The United States Jaycees is made up of three hundred and twenty five thousand young men in more than six thousand chapters. Through their Operation Threshold, they have tried to create an awareness and understanding about alcohol and alcoholism especially for young people. They respect the individual's decision to drink or not to drink. They say: "Responsible drinking can be honorable, safe, healthy, and sensible, and reflects alcohol's use for the enjoyment of life rather than a crutch against it. It involves intention and attitude more than just correct mechanical things. In a deeper sense it may reveal your personal outlook on life. And your personal outlook on life takes into account your upbringing, value system, life style, religious feeling, age, maturity, experiences, living skills, and responsibility. In the final analysis, anyone choosing to drink has a responsibility not to destroy himself or society."

chapter 15

Behavior Modification

One great hope for the future in overcoming such bad habits as overeating, oversmoking, and overdrinking lies in behavior modification techniques. The father of behaviorial psychiatry was a Russian physiologist, Ivan Pavlov, whose work was carried on by B.F. Skinner and others. Drinking is a conditioned response, the behaviorists believe, and the alcoholic is rewarded in certain ways for his drinking behaviors. The principle is that behavior that is positively reinforced will be repeated. Nancy Mello and other behaviorists believe alcoholics drink to relieve anxiety and that this relief constitutes its own reinforcement, this seeming quality of immediate gratification.

Behavior modification is relatively new. Only in the past thirty years have experimentally derived concepts been used to change maladaptive behavior patterns in an organized, systematic way. The field represents an extension of the basic research on animal learning (as begun by Pavlov and Skinner) to problems of human behavior. This approach relates to the measurable response to stimuli. Two important concepts have evolved out of this approach: "contingency management" and "stimulus control."

Contingency management relates to the observation that consequences of behavior determine future behavior. Thus, a behavior which has been reinforced is more likely to be repeated again. A reward such as praise, payment, or a gift is an example of a positive reinforcer. Stimulus control provides the context for ongoing behavior. An analysis of stimulus control shows how the environment in many behaviorial situations may control behavior. Typically, a detailed record is kept showing current mood, location, social situation, and other defining characteristics surrounding the maladaptive behavior, such as drinking excessively.

Applications of behaviorial concepts to human problems began in the area of alcoholism, mental retardation, neurosis, and psychosis. Behavior modification techniques have also been used successfully in dealing with such diverse problems as chronic pain, hysteria, depression, stuttering, phobias, and poor study habits. In behavior modification techniques, the importance of self-control is emphasized. With self-control methods, the passive role of patient is transformed into an active one as participant. The role of therapist is changed from doctor to coach, motivating behavior change, outlining different techniques for improvement, and applauding improved behavior.

While some of the jargon used in behavioral therapy may seem complicated, the principle is very simple: for instance, the using of an alarm clock to wake up on time in the morning is a self-control strategy to elicit a certain kind of desired behavior. In a like manner, as Dr. Ovide Pomerleau (of the Center for Behavioral Medicine at the University of Pennsylvania, Philadelphia, Pennsylvania), has pointed out "strategies can be devised to modify maladaptive habits so as to minimize long-range negative consequences; for example, self-control tactics may be used to increase control over a drinking habit, thereby avoiding alcoholism as an ultimate aversive consequence."

He believes that self-control procedures in which people change their own behavior to achieve certain long-range goals or advantages seem more likely to succeed than those that attempt to modify behavior by simply trying to control or remove misuse substances from the environment, as is demonstrated by the lack of success in legislating self-control by raising the price of cigarettes through taxation, or by prohibiting the sale of alcohol.

Common disorders of self-control include oversmoking, overdrinking, and overeating, each having a common bond of orality. Behavior modification techniques make it possible to consider all three within a common framework of abusive behavior requiring modification through self-control. Among the recent trends in the treatment of overdrinking has been an increasing reliance on rewarding good behavior, rather than punishing bad (shock treatments, Antabuse); the use of behavioral contracts to enhance a client's commitment to a particular goal of treatment, and the idea that controlled drinking is as feasible a goal for some alcoholics as abstinence.

Dr. Bill Miller of the University of New Mexico writes of the new behavioral control techniques: "One particularly promising strategy entails the training of clients in basic self-control. Procedures including self-monitoring and the functional analysis of drinking behavior." Dr. Miller reported that clients treated by this method showed significant decreases in drinking, and were no less improved than another group receiving considerably more extensive treatment. At the one-year follow-up, 78% of the clients receiving behavioral self-control training were still considered successful. At the Palo Alto Veterans Hospital, twenty-nine alcoholics entered classes for those desiring greater self-control in drinking. These lasted about ninety minutes and closely followed the content organization of the textbook of Miller and Munoz, *How To Control Your Drinking*, which presented the following sequence:

1. Overview of the course and specific goal setting.
2. Rate control training.
3. Training in self-reinforcement.
4. Introduction to stimulus control principles.
5. Functional analysis of drinking.
6. Individual consultations regarding present progress.
7. Introduction to alternatives to drinking.
8. Progressive relaxation training.
9. Assertiveness and communication skills.
10. Final assessment and course evaluation.

The results of the ten-week course were based on clients' drinking behavior obtained from three sources: (1) clients' self-report during interviews, (2) clients' daily record cards, and (3) reports from significant others.

In his investigations, Dr. Miller found that group behavior therapy was found to successfully produce controlled drinking in 70% of clients treated. Participants reported that they had benefitted greatly from their interaction with each other. Many expressed their opinion that a self-help program without the motivation of a group or therapist would not have been as effective for them. It was Dr. Miller's impression that the clients for whom the program was least effective were those whose drinking was most deeply embedded in what might be called "neurotic behavior." He conceded that problem drinkers showing more overt signs of anxiety and depression or those who have long used alcohol as a coping mechanism for a variety of stressful life situations may well require more than self-control training directed at drinking behavior.

Behavioral treatment techniques are coming into vogue especially in dealing with veterans. (It is a well known fact that many war veterans have alcohol and drug problems.) For the most part young veterans (from twenty-one to thirty-five years) are increasingly asking for help with a drinking problem, and many are not willing to accept the total abstinence treatment. At the Veterans Administration Center, Jackson, Mississippi, they have initiated a multifaceted behavior therapy program designed to teach responsible drinking to veterans. It focuses on five points teaching (1) social drinking skills, (2) alcohol facts and education, (3) self-management skills, (4) contingency management, rearranging the consequences of drinking, and (5) teaching other social skills and maintenance of responsible drinking over a long period of time.

While no request for abstinence-oriented treatment is ever denied, those wishing to learn to drink moderately there are freely helped to their objective. These patients are given access to alcoholic beverages in a simulated living room setting. Components of social drinking are taught, via specific instructions, performance feedback, social reinforcement from the therapist, and behavioral rehearsal. Patients are taught, for example, always to mix drinks (no straight alcohol), to use a shot glass to measure the amount in each drink, to take small sips, to increase the inter-sip interval (time between drinks), and to limit intake to two drinks on any one occasion. Drinking sessions are videotaped.

Dr. Peter Miller, who has done a very interesting paper on *Training Responsible Drinking With Veterans*, makes the point that "in many cases the young veteran must either choose this (traditional abstinence oriented) treatment or receive no help at all. Controlled drinking treatment has the advantage of being attractive to younger veterans and also serves to lessen the likelihood that they will develop a more chronic alcoholic pattern." The ability to have one or two drinks and then refuse more can be learned, just as any other drinking behavior.

At the Veterans Hospital, University of Mississippi Medical Center, Jackson, Mississippi, veterans are taught to effectively refuse drinks against peer pressure to drink. Appropriate refusals include: (1) looking directly at the person, (2) getting an appropriate affect (i.e., looking and sounding like you really mean it), (3) changing the subject, (4) offering an alternative ("No, thanks, but I would like a glass of iced tea"), and (5) requesting a change in the person's behavior ("I'm trying to cut down on my drinking so please don't ask me to have any more").

Self-management skills of self-control consist of thinking up responses to decrease the likelihood of excessive drinking. This might involve keeping the liquor cabinet supplies low, putting the bottle back after each drink, allowing others to mix their own drinks to avoid "pushing" drinks, thinking through situations which might trigger excesses, such as ways of handling rejection in a nonself-destructive manner.

Here are some other points alcoholic veterans were told to consider: (1) eating prior to drinking slows down the absorption of alcohol, (2) the effects of alcohol may depend on your mood, and (3) alcohol is absorbed less quickly when carbonated beverages are not used.

One of the goals of alternatives training and behavioral counseling is to encourage drinkers not to drink alone or with companions that would urge them to drink to excess. A change from drinking alone or drinking in bars to drinking only when out to dinner with moderate drinking friends would be considered an improvement in "drinking management."

Videotapes of drunken behavior showed to sober alcoholics is aversive to most; however, it should be pointed out that the typical stress reaction is to drink. As Dr. Roger E. Vogler has noted: "While videotaped feedback alone might not generate a positive change in drinking habits, it might be used to generate a strong motivation for change. If this motivation were immediately channeled into a highly structured program, one of the major stumbling blocks to most therapeutic approaches, the ambivalence of the individual to commit himself to change might be overcome. The ability to motivate alcoholics to change is important; because many alcoholics, particularly those who are court referred, are not likely to participate actively and cooperatively in any treatment program."

Self-assertion training has proved valuable to overdrinkers. Mark and Linda Sobell have told how, for some subjects, follow-up has disclosed that effects of the stimulus control sessions have been much more than learning how to handle specific situations. "In particular, subjects who were found to be functioning well after discharge seemed to have experienced a more general form of learning, sometimes called rule learning or learning-to-learn."

They told of an "on the wagon" experimental subject who was able to analyze an experienced desire to drink as resulting from the fact that his brother was living in his house, freeloading off him and attempting to seduce his wife. The subject was able to consider a number of options for his response behavior, including migrating to Chicago. After analyzing the various alternatives in terms of long-range consequences, he decided upon confronting his brother and demanding that he move out.

To the subject's amazement, his brother moved out and his marriage relationship improved considerably thereafter. He had no need to pick up a drink and act in a self-destructive manner because of the actions of other people, which some alcoholics claim is what motivates them to overdrink. Learning to handle the provocative behavior of other people is important, as one drinker put it: "I won't let *them* drive me to drink!"

A response of overdrinking is conceived as having been acquired because the problem drinker has at one time found in it some reward or satisfaction, consciously or unconsciously. As Mark and Linda Sobell have noted, among the possible rewarding consequences which could result from heavy drinking in a stressful situation are:

1) Alcohol, being an effective sedative could offer temporary escape from a disturbing situation. This could also have a detaining effect on certain aggressive behaviors. (A passive-aggressive syndrome has often been noted in male alcoholics.)

2) Alcohol, consumed in large quantities, is physically debilitating, which would permit the drinker to avoid participating in many situations which, for whatever reasons, he finds unpleasant or undesirable. The sedative nature of the binge drinking could reduce the magnitude of anxiety states.

3) Alcohol intoxication is socially accepted as an excuse for engaging in certain otherwise inappropriate behavior, such as extreme flirtation, aggression, homosexuality, etc. The opportunity to engage in certain behavior with a minimum of chastisement acts as a reinforcer for certain drinking behavior in some people.

While stress reduction is probably the primary use of excessive drinking, researchers have noted other powerful reinforcers of overdrinking such as medical and psychiatric care, increased attention, money, an excuse for failures of all sorts, welfare, rehabilitation programs, concern of family and friends, guidance and counseling services. One researcher noted that some alcoholics will come into treatment, remaining sober only until they receive certain monetary benefits from it, such as new dentures, job reinstatement, etc.

Basically behavior change training sessions as defined by Mark and Linda Sobell, incorporate four stages: (1) *Problem Identification*. Define specific circumstances which might be likely to precipitate abusive drinking; (2) *Alternative Responses to Drinking*. Ways in which a person can respond to stress situation without use of alcohol. (3) *Evaluation of Alternatives*. (4) *Exercising the Best Alternative*. Most important is choosing and exercising the response that is at least self-destructive in terms of long-range consequences.

Rather than classifying their clients as "drunk" or "sober," drinking behavior is assessed according to "daily drinking disposition," which is categorized as (1) abstinent—no drinking; (2) controlled drinking, consumption of six ounces or less of 86 proof liquor or its equivalent; (3) drunk, consumption of greater than six ounces of 86 proof alcohol or equivalent; (4) hospitalized for alcohol related problem; and (5) jailed for alcohol related reasons.

While scientific evidence has proven that some alcoholics can control their drinking, a note of caution should be sounded, especially for older chronic types, brainwashed in AA dogma about how alcoholics are supposed to behave. As Mark and Linda Sobell have said: "Certainly the pattern of moderate drinking acquired by former alcoholics is a special kind of drinking. Reinhardt and Bowen have suggested the term 'controlled drinker' to identify such persons. By their definition, the 'controlled drinker,' unlike the normal or social drinker, must be on guard, must choose carefully and even compulsively the time, the place, and the circumstances of drinking and he or she must rigidly limit the amount he or she drinks."

chapter 16

Techniques for Solitary Self-Help

What can you do all by yourself to conquer your drinking problem? A lot. You'll have to get to know a stranger, yourself, a lot better. And you'll have to take him or her in hand—and be your own best friend. You'll have to talk to yourself, reason, even argue with yourself in those inner conversations of the mind. Whether your goal is abstinence or controlled drinking, you'll need to get insight into yourself, how you stand with other people, your relationship to the world around you—and how much you believe in yourself.

First, the person who wants to control his drinking should get a notebook or diary and begin to record every drop of liquor consumed, along with the day, date, situation, and pertinent remarks. In the back of the notebook you might jot down such comments as: "What I don't like about my drinking," "The things I enjoy about drinking," "Does drinking improve or downgrade the person I want to be," and "What are the consequences of my drinking both positively and negatively." Think carefully before you drink so that you can make mature decisions regarding "how much" based on self-respect and respect for others.

As Morris Chafetz has written: "What is generally not understood is that there is a safe way to drink. In terms of amount, it is the equivalent of about one and one-half ounces of absolute alcohol per day. That would be three one-ounce drinks of 100 proof whiskey (which should be diluted) or four eight-ounce glasses of beer or a half bottle of table wine." You say you can't even get a buzz on with that? My suggestion: then drink champagne as due to its bubbliness, it packs more of a wallop per gram of alcohol contained than anything else.)

When it comes to achieving an objective, small things can be a big help. Sometimes it is some little idea, a piece of advice, a hint, that makes all the difference. One person said that the use of a one hour timer helped her to space her drinks not more frequently than one hour apart. Other hints on controlled drinking include: always mix your own drinks and measure on the skimpy side (no doubles); dilute your drinks with lots of water or ice (the art of hydrolution); take small sips and increase your intersip interval (time between sips) every other drink; have a nonalcoholic beverage; eat a meal before drinking or drink (wine) during the meal. Stay away from too much coffee, as it can make you nervous.

Some other suggestions include socializing only with abstainers or moderate drinkers, scheduling alternative activities for times you might be tempted to overdrink such as Friday or Saturday nights. Don't bring a bottle home if you are prone to overdrink in solitude. Train yourself to appreciate quality over quantity. Buy good stuff and be very stingy with it. Don't take a drink to the phone. Always put the bottle back in the liquor cabinet so that each time you have to make a special trip to get more. Take vitamins and eat well.

Always use the glass appropriate to what you are drinking. Eat healthful snacks between drinks such as celery and cream cheese. Don't drink before going to a cocktail party. Don't try to sustain a high. Don't let anyone rush you when you are drinking, especially bartenders who are inclined to push drinks. if you are thirsty, quench your thirst with a glass of water before drinking alcohol. See that you underdrink rather than outdrink those around you. I once asked Barbra Streisand in an interview why she didn't drink (or only very sparingly), to which she replied, "I never like to be out of control." It's a thought.

Watch for signs you may be nearing your cutoff point. Don't drink to help you tolerate boring people, instead leave them and find some who are not. Never drink while doing business, it may cloud your judgment. Don't use alcohol to put yourself to sleep: try a cup of warm milk and honey. Make no commitments regarding marriage, sex, or money while drinking. Don't sign anything if you've had so much as one drink. Don't let other people influence you to have another, if you've had enough. Never drink because it's a freebie.

Find out your limit—and stay within that limit. Plan your time so that drinking is on the periphery of your life, rather than in central focus. Find alternatives to drinking. Never drink around the clock—drinking has a time and a place. Don't use your liquor store as your bank. Never start a tab. Buy small quantities of liquor and keep your liquor cabinet locked. Be satisfied with a slight mellow feeling. Never drink to get drunk. Don't use booze for an aphrodisiac or pain killer. Drink only with meals. Never drink on an empty stomach.

If you usually have two or three drinks at lunch, cut down to one. Set aside dry days each week, perhaps alternating with slightly wet days. Set the cocktail hour as late as possible in the day or eliminate the cocktail hour. Become a connoisseur of fine wines and spirits. Stop buying the cheap house brand. Get interested in wine tasting and learn the correct way. If you are going out to supper, plan in advance (and work your plan) just how many drinks you'll have. You'll find you'll be very pleased with yourself when you've done what you said you were going to do.

The way you drink is significant. In AA they say: "An alcoholic drinks in a way so as to become drunk." Dr. Mark Sobell identified from his studies certain characteristics of heavy drinkers or alcoholics. He found that alcoholic subjects generally ordered straight drinks, while normal drinkers preferred mixed drinks; alcoholics generally gulped their drinks, no matter what type of drink was being consumed and drank much faster than the normal drinkers; alcoholics sipped less frequently than normal drinkers.

Drinking charts have been found useful for those who don't like diaries. All drinking should be accurately reported as to time, place, and amount. Next, the drinking experience should be analyzed in terms of consequences, which actually or could potentially have occurred, with special emphasis on long-term consequences; and the attainment of target goals both in regard to drinking and life-functioning values.

Day	Date	Situation	Consumption	Remarks
Sat.	8/21/77	More tasks than I can handle.	$5^1/_3$ oz. sherry	Slept poorly, many dreams.
Sun.	8/22/77	Spent 3 hours canvassing people in neighborhood. Worked hard to clean up rooms.	2½ oz. brandy $1^1/_3$ oz. gin 2 oz. white wine	I was too tired and upset to handle the amount and I think I *drank too much.*
Mon.	8/23/77	Close friend who takes up time and energy and is not sympathetic came over.	1 beer.	Managed to get rid of friend and cut the lawn without over drinking!

Any overdrinking should be underlined in red pencil. Descriptions of situations and remarks can be much more detailed. The author of this chart says that her drinking pattern starts when she gets home from work and continues while cooking dinner. "After that," she says, "I quit!" I guess I really do use alcohol as a relaxant." She has found two things of major assistance to her (other than meetings):

1) Tea. "I experiment with different kinds and have five or six varieties always on hand."

2) Record faithfully every ounce or fraction of an ounce of alcoholic beverages on the chart and do this while you are drinking, after pouring the drink but before consuming it. And in between drinks, drink lots of tea.

One thing let us remember: to cut down or quit drinking, it is not necessary to *do* but necessary to *not do* something (picking up a drink). You must get over the idea that any degree of deprivation is unbearable. You must choose the greater good over the not so good. You have to get over the idea that it is "not fair that I can't drink with abandon," and say to yourself "the reason I have to carefully watch it now is that I overdrank in the past." You can have the pleasurable taste sensation you enjoy, but only in moderation. Behavior change will occur when and only when you realize the sentences you are telling yourself such as "I can't stand it without a drink" are discovered, evaluated, and rationally contradicted.

To drink or not to drink is a matter of personal choice and as in every choice, one or more alternatives are relinquished to gain the one selected. This is true of all decisions. (You can't, alas, have your cake and eat it too.) In the same way, your drinking is a personal decision, a matter of choice. The crucial point is: are you going to choose to favor what is best for you, or the opposite? Are you going to lift yourself up or drag yourself down? It's up to you. Never let others drive you to drink.

Dr. Martha Sanchez-Craig has said that: "Our behavior is determined by the way we interpret events. Some events we appraise as having no effect on us, some as being beneficial and others as harmful. When an individual appraises an event as potentially harmful or aversive, his immediate tendency is to react by attack, avoidance, or withdrawal. In relation to alcohol, drinking to excess represents a way of coping with aversion or bad news. Drink may increase a person's confidence to handle the bad news or may be an escape from intolerable events. Thus a bad habit develops. Most overdrinkers have a high degree of ambiviance about their drinking: they know it would better if they didn't abuse alcohol (and themselves), but it may be the only one of a few alternatives for coping with a depressing set of life circumstances. His success in stopping abusing alcohol may depend on first identifying the 'precipating event' or emotion, sorrow, boredom, guilt, anger, that caused the spree."

The alcoholic must appraise his situation in a new way which means redefining his thinking. He can catastrophize the happening. He can look up to it as a mountain or cut it down to the size of an anthill by the way he interprets it. (For instance, if a loved one deserts him, he can say: "I've been betrayed again. I need a drink." Or, he can redefine the situation and say something like, "Well, if that's the kind of person she is, I'm well rid of her. She did me a favor by leaving. Anyway, I can handle the situation without getting bombed.")

You can cope with any situation without alcohol. Just don't drink. Think of alternative coping devices. Actually list them. Also, write down helpful phrases such as: "How foolish I'd be to give in to that desire," or "I am about to make a mistake. I can avoid being that stupid and self-destructive." List ways you'd advise another person (imaginery) who asked for advice on this problem.

Behavior modification concepts can be helpful to you. Behavior modification techniques are more concerned with your behavior rather than how you think, feel, or what motivates you. The behaviorists say behavior is controlled by reinforcement—either positive or negative. Good consequences are positive; bad, negative. Negative reinforcement doesn't produce desired behavior but it can help extinguish an undesirable one. You must begin to reward your good behavior; for instance, if you've been abstinent for several weeks, as was your goal, take yourself out to dinner or a show.

Behavior "contracting" in its simplest form is that you bet someone something you can stay sober for a month and he bets you something that you can't. You can also make "contracts" with yourself; and it will do your self-esteem much good to see that you honor them. In other words, you make a commitment, and honor the commitment.

If you feel in need of extra support, the "buddy" system can be enormously helpful, especially if you can find somebody local who is working on the same goal you are. Get a copy of the Miller and

Munoz book, *How To Control Your Drinking*, and read every word. If you still feel you need help, you might consider therapy or joining a self-help group. But I can assure you, it's possible to do it all by yourself. (Perhaps not as easily, but it can be done.) You don't need a complete character change to moderate your drinking. It's quite simple: the key to moderate drinking is knowing when to stop.

L. Davis reported in a study of ninety-three alcohol addicts some years ago that seven of them returned to normal drinking (after a period of abstinence) without problems. He particularly noted that none of these men had received a therapeutic reconstruction of their "core" personalities, which at the time was thought to be necessary.

How can you control the effects of alcohol? No two people, unfortunately, react exactly the same way to ethyl alcohol; but we can make some valid generalizations. Alcohol, after finding its way into the blood stream, begins to work on the central nervous system and may slow down brain activity. It can cause a release of inhibitions and, eventually, affect motor centers of the brain. (Musicians, even mildly intoxicated, will be unable to play the piano well.) As drinking continues, slurred speech will develop, vision becomes impaired, and walking straight becomes an impossibility.

The speed at which alcohol affects motor centers of the brain varies due to many factors. Food slows down the process. Drinking wine with a meal is far less harmful than drinking whiskey on an empty stomach. Timing, as in all else, is a crucial factor. An average person can burn off an ounce of 86 proof whiskey in an hour or less. Many experts agree that one or two drinks a day won't cause you any significant harm, even if consumed over a period of years. But more than that, medical experts say, could cause your liver to become fatty, especially if you don't eat right and get proper nutrition. Taking no more than two single drinks a day, they say, is okay. So get into the habit, if you drink, of saying no to that third drink.

Like any drug, alcohol's effect depends in part on your body's weight: the lighter you are, the greater the effect of any given amount. Alcohol is metabolized by the liver at the fixed rate of about one ounce per hour. To achieve a blood alcohol level of .05, a person of one hundred pounds could only have one drink; whereas, a person of one hundred and eighty pounds could have three. The four drinks that will make a one hundred pound person drunk will have little effect on the person weighing two hundred pounds, who will require eight for the same effect.

Of the many investigators who have reported successfully training alcoholics to control their drinking, some indicate that an important element was that patients learn to monitor their own behavior. The use of the *Mobat* has been helpful to many. This is an inexpensive, portable test for determining blood alcohol concentration (BAC). Originally, these BAC machines were developed to meet the needs of the criminal justice system in prosecuting those caught driving while under the influence of alcohol. The ones used in the court, however, are heavy, cumbersome, nonportable, highly sophisticated, and expensive and not at all suited to the individual needs of the home drinker.

Thus, the *Mobat* (mobile breath alcohol test) was developed in the 1970s by the Luckey Laboratories, Inc., 7252 Osburn Road, San Bernardino, California 92404. It is a screening test in which a specified volume of mixed, expired breath is passed through a tube containing a dry silica, treated with specific chemicals. The *Mobat* has three distinct yellow rings that turn green as the result of interacting with alcohol in the breath. The rings indicate ranges of BAC from 0.00 to 0.30. The *Mobat* is easy to use and inexpensive. (Cost is from $2.50 to $3.00, depending on the quantity ordered, so that the price per test runs about $ .50.)

An important point is that the *Mobat* is self-contained and needs no laboratory analysis. With its low cost and high degree of portability, drinkers can get immediate feedback in regard to their own level of intoxication at any time. It can be an important adjunct in self-training to estimate BAC. Drs. Mark and Linda Sobell have stated: "We have never found a false positive reading using the *Mobat*."

Every now and then, even if you are doing great with your moderate drinking program, you'll want to go on the wagon. There are many reasons for abstinence: to clear your mind for business or educational reasons, to save money, for athletics, because you have nondrinkers visiting you, to lose weight, to prepare for a stage debut, to put your body in peak health, to prove you are not dependent on alcohol, etc. The problem is to motivate yourself and understand (and approve) the reasons you aren't imbibing.

Here are some tips for an abstinence regimen. First, don't think that you are depriving yourself of anything but, rather, that you are doing something good for you. If you want something that may give you the illusion of a drink, buy carbonated water. Add lemon and lots of ice. (Get the no-calorie kind—and you can drink literally gallons of it and it won't add a pound of body weight.) It will be a little comfort to you. And you can, if you wish, pretend you are drinking when you are not. (And if you get a craving for alcohol, take a spoonful of honey. It will go away.)

The AA idea: "To stay away from one drink, one day at a time," is a good one. Don't think you have to drink for business or social reasons. You don't. Nobody will care really. Just say: "I'm not drinking right now," or "No alcohol, doctor's orders." You need not explain. Becoming master of yourself and your environment is a heady intoxicant in itself. But beware when things are going too good. That's the danger time, when the mischief maker that lives in the unconscious mind of each one of us may tempt you to ruin everything. Just plain boredom, a lack of adventure or risk taking in your life could lead you on a drinking spree. See that you satisfy these needs in other ways. And watch out for self-destructive power and dependency needs. They can foul you up every time.

And don't, if you use booze, drink for self-medication; but rather as a companion to good food or at a social event. According to the authors of a German program in Sankelmark, Germany: "To abuse alcohol is to drink it because of its action upon one's spirits, to wash away depression, to resolve conflicts or appease anger or to get into a good mood. In other words, the abuse of alcohol is to use it as though it were medicine."

chapter 17

Self-Help Groups
and Inter-Group Dynamics

You could say, of course, that group therapy began as far back as the twelve disciples of Christ. But group therapy, as we know it today, began to be popular in this country in the 1940s and 1950s with a variety of techniques. These include the stimulation of emotional release of members in a supportive setting, the instillation of hope of change, as one observes the improvement of other members of the group combating a similar problem or notices self-improvement and universal feelings are compared and accepted. Some members in certain groups, also, confront each other with negative material and each member gets a chance to sit on the hot seat to face some constructive criticism.

Other group confrontations occur in psychodrama, in which participants act out, in impromptu dramas, a variety of roles which help release their own and others' repressed emotions. Psychodrama has been described by Dr. Sheila B. Blume as a "variety of group therapy that depends on spontaneous and immediate gratification and is a useful adjunct in the rehabilitation of men and women suffering from alcoholism." Dr. Blume is unit chief for alcoholism at Central Islip Hospital, Psychiatric Center, New York, and she was responsible for introducing psychodrama into the hospital's therapeutic curriculum. She finds it most helpful in breaking down barriers and getting through to the shy ones. She says, "Conflicts revealed in a one-to-one, or small group counseling situation are often worked through on the psychodrama stage. Conversely, meaningful episodes that erupt on the psychodrama stage may be explored in depth by a counselor and an individual client."

Dr. J.L. Moreno has been credited with originating psychodrama in 1923. A resident of Vienna, Dr. Moreno emigrated to this country in 1925 and began his work here. He established the

Moreno Institute in Beacon, New York. (Today the school is directed by his widow, Zerka Moreno. It is the only center that fully accredits psychodramatists.) Both Dr. Blume and Hannah B. Weiner were students of Dr. Moreno. Ms. Weiner works at the Center for Experimental Learning in New York City. Psychodrama is great for the imagination and helps drain off hostility feelings.

Ms. Weiner defines psychodrama as "a method of learning through the spontaneous enacting of situations. One or more individuals take the role of themselves in the present, themselves at another time, another person, or as an inanimate object. They explore ideas and situations—verbally and nonverbally—while the rest of the group observes what is happening." The roles may be assigned or chosen and the scenes may involve those that are real or those purely imagined.

Ms. Weiner believes that psychodrama is an excellent technique in working with alcohol addicts. She notes: "The flexibility of the method is a match for the variety of problems, personalities, and situations of the individual with an alcohol problem." Psychodrama is active, rather than passive, and utilizes stage techniques. The therapist becomes the director. Dr. Blume has identified some recurring themes in dealing with alcoholics, such as personifying alcohol itself; identifying with alcoholic parents; preparing the alcoholic for the job interview; and helping patients prepare to face social situations without alcohol.

Transactional analysis, where life is seen as a series of games in which one can play the role of parent or child, is popular today. Claude Steiner, a transactional analyst from San Francisco, in his article: *The Alcoholic Game*, identifies the roles in the alcoholic's game and discusses what the interpersonal advantages are of playing it. He defines the role of the alcoholic's pusher or supplier (such as bartender) and his rescuers and how the game becomes self-perpetuating as each role player has a stake in continuing the game.

Dr. I.D. Yolom of Stanford University says that alcoholics need more attention from the leader of a group than from the other members because of their greater dependency needs. In between group sessions, he permits his clients to continue contact with him by phone or mail. He wholeheartedly believes that behavior can be changed through "alternates of intrapsychic and interpersonal dynamics."

Gestalt therapy is also popular today. In Gestalt therapy, individuals plunge into heated dialogues with themselves in front of a group and try to achieve intense emotional experience in a group setting. Gestalt therapy works to help the patient overcome self-division and become a whole person. Inner dialogues of the mind are revealed, in conversations with one or more personalities within oneself needing integration. The Gestalt center adheres to the techniques of the late Fritz Perls, originator of the "I please myself" approach and the "hot seat," where the patient expresses any thoughts that cross his or her mind in front of group members. (Gestalt Center for Psychotherapy and Training is at 1040 Park Avenue, New York, NY.)

Self-regulation therapy, which involves the use of relaxation training, biofeedback instrumentation, and meditation, is employed as an adjunct to treatment in the Alcoholism Program and Education Center at Loretto Hospital in Chicago, Illinois. Joseph Troiani, Director, says: "self-regulation can be helpful as it teaches a person to manipulate his or her internal environment and, thus, reduce emotional stress without resorting to the use of external agents such as alcohol or tranquilizers."

One of the methods used to induce a state of relaxation in the patient employs the use of the electroencephalograph, an instrument that traces brain wave activity, and the electromyograph which measures muscle response. These instruments signal to the patient the body's response while he or she makes a conscious effort to relax. In the first sessions, the person is taught to relax as deeply as possible through simple, physical means such as comfortable seating, concentration, controlled breathing, and muscle relaxation.

In the second phase, the person joins a group, which is under the supervision of a biofeedback trainer. The trainer leads the group through specific fantasies and daydreams. Research has shown that these guided "inner trips" do more than any single biofeedback technique to help a person move into an altered state of awareness, which is the goal of biofeedback training.

The third phase requires the use of an instrument through which the person learns to move into an "altered state," from the audio or visual feedback provided by the machine. The eighteen-bed facility at Loretto Hospital has twelve full-time staff members and has treated close to three hundred people, since it was opened in 1974. (For further information contact Alcohol Program, Loretto Hospital, 645 S. Central Avenue, Chicago, Illinois 60644.)

Project Intercept began in 1976, for "early stage alcoholics," or overdrinkers. The program is open for all drug dependencies, as it appears that most patients treated combine alcohol with one or more other mood-altering drugs. The usual program is a four-week term of group therapy. "We find that new patients benefit greatly from the experience of meeting with those already in the program," says Dr. Alan Wilson, Director. "Also, individuals vary in the length of time it requires for them to respond to group therapy," he says. Currently the only requirement placed on a referral is that they reside close enough to attend all therapy sessions and that they be able to remain abstinent as they get involved in treatment. Funding may be from private payment, health insurance, Medicare or Medicaid.

Following detoxification, for those who need it, patients are mainly treated with group therapy. "Our patients learn to talk to and listen to other people," says John Reimer, head counselor for the program. "They learn to be happy even if they don't always get their way. They learn openness, honesty with others, responsibility for their own actions. They learn to like themselves. They learn that life isn't automatically good, but that they must make it good." (For more information write: *Intercept*, Dr. Alan Wilson, Director, Outpatient Services, Moraine Hospital, 4839 N. Hewitts Point Road, Oconomowoc, Wisconsin 53066.)

The Association of Drinkwatchers, International, Inc. (DW), was formed in late 1974 as a nonprofit, educational, self-help group which offers a choice of therapeutic goals, either abstinence or controlled drinking, when there are no medical contraindications. Drinkwatchers' aim is to put alcohol in proper focus on the periphery of your life rather than in central focus whether that be abstinention or moderate drinking. Drinkwatchers is not for extreme cases who need hospital detoxification centers, courts, jails, or medical treatment. It is not for people who think they have an incurable disease who are referred to AA.

There are usually two groups working in each DW meeting; those working on abstinence regimens and those wanting to do controlled drinking. Those working on moderate drinking keep a "drink diary" in which they write down the exact amounts of alcohol consumed each day, the situation, and their remarks which include emotional reactions and precipating events. Also included are notations as to time, place, and people involved in each drinking situation. Nutritional factors are important.

Each person fashions, with help, a custom-tailored program for himself or herself. There may be an emphasis on self-assertion training, rational-emotive thinking, constructive rebellion, goal achievement, and behavior modification techniques. Self-control is encouraged. Anhedonia therapy is indicated for the overdrinker with depression. For drinkers an attitude of "connoisseur" is fostered, as the opposite of abusing anything is to treat it with respect and appreciation. In line with this, speakers are invited to meetings, such as an expert on wine tasting or someone from a well-known vineyard. Those who drink are to strive for an attitude toward alcohol comparable to that of the gourmet toward food. DW has a pro-joy attitude.

Drinkwatchers is a learning (or relearning) process. Members can stay as long as they want, until they know enough about alcohol, or can handle it without the supportive group. They can come back any time for a refresher course. The idea is to teach them whatever they want and need to know and then let them rejoin society at large. The whole thrust of the program is to train, or retrain, people to live normally amoung friends, family, neighbors, and business contacts and not be "different." This is done through an interchange of ideas, problem-solving, discussion, lectures, tips, etc.

Emphasis is on the individual. There are no absolutes in DW. No one thing works for everybody. Guilt and hang-ups are freely and openly discussed. Many people drink too much because they can't (or don't think they can) function because of too many inhibitions. DW feels that alcohol is not the solution to problems, although it can cause problems. There is nothing wrong with taking a couple of aspirin for a headache. But you wouldn't take ten or twenty aspirin for a headache; nor should you take aspirin for a broken bone, upset stomach, measles, or dandruff. In short, DW believes that like everything else, alcohol has its place.

DWs do not encourage confessionals or ruminating over past mistakes. After all, mistakes are how we learn. The occasional drunk episode is discussed at meetings, so everybody can learn. The key to moderate drinking is knowing when to stop. This is part of group discussions. Successful drinking experiences are discussed, and ways and means of moderating. DW is not for persons who want to stay drunk or half-drunk all the time. DW is *not* a group of drunks, but a group of people, who, when they drink, are responsible, in control, and socially correct. DW is not for those seeking a social life or a new mate. DW is not a social club, it's a learning process. In fact, it's a training ground for normal, social involvement. DW avoids labeling or the use of denigrating terms like alcoholic.

DW views alcohol as a neutral spirit which only becomes good or bad, depending on how you use it. Those on moderation programs are guided to: "Drink—but not make drink your master." Behavior modification techniques are used. Drinkwatchers can be anonymous if they choose, but need not be. As one DW expressed the idea: "We are as proud of our efforts to control our drinking as another might be of losing weight in some program."

There are three kinds of people that DW wants to help: (1) those just starting to drink (teenagers and some adults) who don't know anything about alcohol and want some information, (2) the social drinker who hasn't had any problems with alcohol as yet and wants to keep it that way, and (3) the so-called problem drinkers who either wishes to abstain for a while or learn to modify his or her drinking habits. While drinking to excess is never condoned, DWs are not made to feel guilty for slips. They are not ever stigmatized.

Dr. Mortimer Hartman, medical advisor to Drinkwatchers says the statement, "Once an alcoholic, always an alcoholic" is false. He says the correct term is abuse, substance abuse. Anything can be abused: people, animals, things, relationships, power, etc. But the cure for abuse is not necessarily abstention. In fact, a person may be greatly demoralized by his inability to control his drinking.

Drinkwatchers is an extended family made up of people with a common interest in alcohol and alcohol problems. DW publishes a monthly newsletter telling of meetings in various places, tips on abstinence or controlled drinking; giving news, views, humor, and poetry. ($12 a year postpaid.) There is also a book available *How To Be A Drinkwatcher*. (For information, write DW, P.O. Box 179, Haverstraw, N.Y. 10927.)

Dr. Andre Boudreau of Canada, who is in charge of a number of programs for alcohol and drug addicts and has been associated with clinics in France, opens "Welcome Halls" for abusers, which are as cordial to newcomers as the name implies. He is particularly interested in the "whys" of drug use and has actually categorized drugs by reasons why people use them, such as "to fight fatigue," "to help me sleep," "to make me feel high," etc.

The Al-Anon program is a fellowship of relatives and friends of alcoholics (who are usually AA members), who hope to solve their own common problems by sharing experiences and increasing knowledge and understanding of themselves and the alcoholic.They try to help the alcoholic by changing their own attitudes and working to provide a healthier environment for the whole family.

They don't believe in "coddling" the overdrinker for they believe "the more help he gets, the less he will do for himself." It is their belief that the alcoholic has an incurable, progressive, terminal disease. They believe that they, too, are sick people. As Bill W. described it: "Alcoholism is a *contagious* disease and you are suffering from its *effects*." The groups are patterned after the AA model and use the AA slogans such as "Easy Does It," "One Step At A Time," and "Keep It Simple." Alateen, an offshoot of Al-Anon, is for the children of alcoholics and also uses the AA model. They try to help each other to learn to detach themselves emotionally from their parent's problems while still retaining love for them.

RUG (Responsible Use Groups) are for people who are experiencing minimal problems related to alcohol and other drug use, as well as those who are not experiencing problems—and simply wish to keep it that way. RUG provides the structure within which drug use patterns can be examined and responsible use can be explored. An underlying belief is that individuals are responsible for their own behavior, and that if an individual chooses to use alcohol or other drugs, it should be done in a way which is enhancing and not destructive. The general objectives of each group RUG are:

1) To help the participants examine their current patterns of alcohol or other drug use.
2) To help participants define for themselves what is responsible use.
3) To help each participant develop reasonable, measurable, responsible use goals.
4) To help participants use the learning experiences offered through RUG to reach individual goals.

They believe the problem, for most of us, is not whether or not to use mood-altering substances (since most of us do), but whether or not to use them responsibly. In addition to goal-setting, examples of learning experiences include assertion-training, valuing, feedback exercises, anger contacts, psychology of intoxication, role-playing, and rational-behavioral techniques. Each Responsible Use Group consists of no more than ten participants and meets once a week for twelve weeks. (Fees are charged on a sliding schedule, based upon ability to pay. For further information, contact Judi Gordon, R.N., or Doug Morgan, Co-directors, RUG, 430 Oak Grove, Minneapolis, minnesota 55403.)

Responsible Drinkers (RD), P.O. Box 1062, Burlingame, California 94010, is a breakaway group from Drinkwatchers on the west coast. RD rejects the disease concept of alcoholism, as well as many myths surrounding the use of alcohol. They try to recognize alcohol in its true context: it is a food, relaxant, mood elevator, social equalizer; it is also a drug and a poison. They believe that when the powers of the drug are not respected, alcohol is a depressant, an anesthetic . . . a problem. Those who have joined and remained with the RD program, they say, are experiencing ever increasing success in dealing with their alcohol related problems. Richard Hull is the leader of the group, which meets weekly.

chapter 18

On Mastering a Drinking Problem

The criteria for mastering a drinking problem can be varied. If one sets up a goal of total abstinence for life, success cannot be measured until the end of life; therefore, AA people wisely advised alcoholics to have as their goal merely "staying away from one drink, one day at a time." When the goal is moderation or controlled drinking, can one consider the day successful if there was no drinking or only trouble-free drinking? Yet the term "trouble-free" is negative. If the person doesn't get any more out of it than avoiding trouble, it hardly seems worthwhile to drink. There should be a plus factor. The drinking should be a pleasurable occasion, perhaps a before-dinner cocktail with friends or some wine with dinner.

The aim of any program of controlled drinking should be at first, of course, to stop the excess, which must be considered as a form of self-destructive activity. (Thus getting smashed is really masochistic.) Anhedonia therapy concerns getting more healthy pleasure out of life. The word *hedone* is from the Greek meaning pleasure and also from *hedys* meaning pleasant or sweet. In psychology, hedonia relates to pleasurable and unpleasurable states of mind. So, if one is going to drink, one should try to cultivate a "gourmet" attitude toward drinking. One should attempt to develop a connoisseur's taste for what is good, rather than doing the guzzling of the alcoholic who hardly knows what he is drinking. You can educate your taste buds. You can induce your mind to a pleasurable state.

Dr. Hartman has stated: "It is not enough for the drinker to stop drinking or learn to moderate. He (or she) has to switch from a loser's lifestyle to that of a winner, as he (or she) defines it." This means fitting alcohol (whether drinking or not) into a larger pattern of successful life functionings.

If one can achieve a happy balance in the areas of love, work, and play, one should be able to fit in some moderate drinking, without making a problem of it. No matter what your age, it is very important to always have some goals before you, even if your goal is to make enough money so you can do nothing. So whatever you'd really like to do in life, focus on your goals. And then press on. And on. Don't acknowledge defeat.

Once you get your body in tip-top shape from good nutrition, plenty of exercise, and deep breathing, you'll be full of energy. (Strangely enough, when your body isn't toxic, you won't want to take into it toxic materials.) Not only will you not experience any craving, you'll wonder what all the fuss was about. You'll have one or two drinks and that will be enough. No question about it. Or you'll need more training.

Dr. R.E. Vogler's program emphasizes discrimination training so that the drinker is aware of his exact *degree* of alcohol intake. The videotape of drunken behavior is to create motivation and the educational part of the program reorients the drinker's thinking about being able to develop moderation skills. A person on his own, could use the ideas suggested here. Ask yourself: Am I aware of how I *feel* at different levels of blood-alcohol concentration? am I highly motivated to change? Do I believe I can drink in a moderate or controlled manner?

If we don't take the reins of self-management, decision-making, and autonomy, they may be taken from us. Once we have begun to take charge of our lives, we don't need to ask others permission to do things. We have internalized the "good parents" we possibly never had. We are able to take responsibility for our lives and for those around us, in the sense of doing nothing harmful to them and in being caring and considerate. Change is not just liberating our true self.

Psychologist Robert W. White says: "Change is never so simple. What is really involved is not the releasing of a true self, but the making of a new self, one gradually transcends the limitations and pettiness of the old. This can only be done by behaving differently when interacting with other people. New strategies have to be evolved that express the new intentions and encourage others to take their reciprocal part in finer human relations."

The development of self-management techniques puts you in control; but that need not mean functioning rigidly. You cannot control circumstances and other people, but you can control yourself and your responses to them. What needs to be developed is what the psychologist Abraham Maslow referred to as self-belief.

Such people, he suggested, can enjoy change because they feel whatever happens, they can handle the situation creatively. They can improvise confidently. They can tolerate higher levels of ambiguity, tension, and insecurity because they are sure of their own capabilities. They have self-belief. As George and Nena O'Neill wrote in their fine book, *Shifting Gears*, "Self-management bolsters the meaning and value of self—and a fuller sense of self-competence is the result."

Many people overdrink to release themselves from feelings of tension. According to the Menninger Clinic, people who control their tensions may be said to be mentally healthy. The Menninger Clinic believes that these people have five characteristics: (1) They are flexible under stress, (2) they treat others as individuals, (3) they obtain gratification from a number of sources such as ideas people, tasks, outside interests, (4) they accept their own capacities and limitations and are realistic in their own self-concepts, and (5) they stay active and productive in the interest of their own fulfillment and in the service of others.

As a healthy person, of course, you won't let your appetites run your life. Cicero wisely observed: "The mind should direct, the appetite obey." You developed a bad habit if you overdrank consistently. Bad habits can be changed to good. Moderation is a learned response, the behavioral scientists tell us. According to Willard and Marguerite Beecher writing in their book, *Beyond Success and Failure*, "Addictions are nothing more than exaggerated habits which we inflate to hide the shallowness of our inner life, our lack of independence, and self-sufficiency. We use them to ward off loneliness. Addictions are props for lagging self-esteem and always are distress signals of a dying initiative."

Develop short and long-range personal goals that are meaningful to you—and don't be overly dependent on other people. Dr. Ari Keiv once wrote in an article: "observing the lives of people who have mastered adversity, I have noted that they have established goals and sought with all their effort to achieve them. From the moment they decided to concentrate all their energies on a specific objective, they began to surmount the most difficult odds." Define your goal and you have taken the first step toward achieving it.

He advises you not to be afraid of failure. Focus on one objective at a time. And always have the next goal in the back of your mind. Your brain, like a servomechanism when set on a target, will call into play those mental processes that can bring your efforts to fruition. Be determined. And don't get impatient. According to an English music critic: "The greatest composer does not set to work because he is inspired; but he becomes inspired because he is working."

If anger develops, Dr. Keiv suggests you review carefully what has happened. Monitor your behavior . . . and that of others. Has somebody criticized you? Must you depend on others' opinions? Have you allowed others to impose their expectations on you? If others aren't treating you right, is that any reason for you to treat yourself badly by overdrinking? Have you no identify of your own worth respecting?

"Self-reliance," says Dr. Keiv, "comes from a positive orientation toward goals and a reduction of unnecessary and inhibiting dependency needs." He also believes that your ability to withdraw into solitude will increase your faith in your capacity to achieve objectives and give you strength to endure frustrations and uncertainty. The lawyer John Foster wrote: "One of the strongest characteristics of genius is the power to light your own fire."

So light your own fire. Take command of your life and habits. You alone can change yourself. You alone can make a firm decision for growth and progress. You alone are the central point of reference for your life. And out of this can come greater strength and confidence leading you away from an unhappy, self-destructive life to one more happy, healthy and rewarding. You will come to control not only your drinking, but all facets of your life.

What we are against is self-hurting excesses. Yet there is a good side to drinking. We're talking about the benefits of moderate amounts of alcohol in a proper social setting. While we do not say alcohol can cure what ails you, there have been some men who praised alcohol enthusiastically. Louis Pasteur said: "Wine is the most hygenic and most healthful of beverages." And Winston Churchill said to his wife, when admonished for the amount he drank: "Clemmie, I have taken more out of alcohol, than alcohol has taken out of me."

Alcohol in the form of wine is one of the oldest medicines. Hippocrates, a celebrated Greek physician used it to fight infection. Ivan Pavlov used it to stimulate appetite. The Persian king, Cyrus the Great, took it along on his marches to avoid diseases caused by impure water. The Jewish physician Maimonides used it as an aid to digestion. Theoricus, a 16th century German, exclaimed: "Alcohol sloweth old age."

Dr. Robert C. Stepto writing in *Chicago Medicine* noted about wine: "Among its half dozen vitamins, vitamin B is most important, occurring in significant amounts, so that wine can be considered a supplementary source. Among the fifteen or twenty minerals present in wine is iron, 80% of which is in the ferrous form that is readily absorbed by the body."

And if sometime you feel you drank more than you should, forget about the error and get back on your regimen. As William Blake observed: "The road of excess leads to the palace of wisdom." Make a list of the gains to you from no excessive use of alcohol. And every once in a while give your body a complete rest from alcohol in the form of a week or two or a month without this toxicity. So that your body, as well as your house, may enjoy the benefits of "spring cleaning."

Dr. Salvador Didato, well-known medical reporter for the Gannett newspaper chain wrote: "People can abuse anything; money, sex, love, friendship, food, etc., but the cure for abuse is not necessarily abstinence. It seems to make more psychological sense to urge certain personalities to drink in moderation rather than have them become demoralized by their own inability to overcome their compulsive drive to drink."

So it is worth it to be able to learn to moderate your habits, that you may have the option to abstain or do controlled drinking as a personal choice. To drink and not make drink your master (or to abstain as you will . . .). A poet has written that one of life's greatest pleasures is "to enjoy good wine in good company." Wrote Leo Tolstoy: "Man is meant for happiness and this happiness is in him, in the satisfaction of the daily needs of his existence."

SUGGESTED FURTHER READING

Alcoholism: The Nutritional Approach, Roger Williams, University of Texas, 1973.

American Drinking Practices, Don Cahalon, Ira H. Cisin, Helen M. Crossley, Rutgers Center of Alcohol Studies, 1969.

Behavioral Treatment of Alcoholism, Peter M. Miller, Pergamon International Library, 1977.

Bombed, Buzzed, Smashed, or Sober, John Langone, Little, Brown, 1976.

Drink to Your Health, Junius Adams, Harpers, 1976.

Drinking in the French Culture, Roland Sandoun, Giorio Lolli, Milton Silverman, Rutgers Center of Alcohol Studies, 1976.

Emerging Concepts of Alcohol Dependence, E. Mansell Pattison, Mark and Linda Sobell, Springer, 1977.

Firewater Myths, Joy Leland, Rutgers Center of Alcohol Studies, 1976.

How to Control Your Drinking, William Miller, Prentice Hall, 1976.

Megavitamin Therapy, Ruth Adams and Frank Murray, Larchmont Books, 1973.

Psychodietetics, Dr. E. Cheraskin and Arline Drecher, Stein and Day, 1976.

To Your Health, Richard S. Shore and John M. Luce, Seabury, 1976.

Why Drinking Can Be Good For You, Morris Chafetz, Stein and Day, 1976.

SOURCES OF FURTHER HELP AND INFORMATION

Addictions Research Foundation
33 Russell St.
Toronto 179, Ontario, Canada

Alcohol and Drug Problems Association of North America
1130 Seventeen St., NW
Washington, D.C. 20036

Alcoholics Anonymous
P.O. Box 459, Grand Central Station
New York, N.Y. 10017

Al-Anon Family Group Headquarters
P.O. Box 182, Madison Sq. Station
New York, N.Y. 10010

American Red Cross Alcohol Program
17th and D St.
Washington, D.C. 20006

Alcohol and Drug Problems Association of North America
1130 Seventeen St., NW
Washington, D.C. 20036

Association of Drinkwatchers, International, Inc.
P.O. Box 179
Haverstraw, N.Y. 10927

Distilled Spirits Council of the U.S.
1300 Pennsylvania Blvd.
Washington, D.C.

National Association of Private Psychiatric Hospitals
353 Broad Ave.
Leonia, N.J. 07605

National Council on Alcoholism
2 Park Ave.,
New York, N.Y. 10016

National Institute on Alcohol Abuse and Alcoholism
5600 Fishers Lane
Rockville, Md. 20852

Responsible Drinkers
P.O. Box 1062
Burlingame, Ca. 90410

Responsible Use Groups
430 Oak Grove
Minneapolis, Mn. 55403

Rutgers Center of Alcohol Studies
Rutgers University
New Brunswick, N.J. 08903

Salvation Army
120 W. 14th St.
New York, N.Y. 10011

United States Jaycees
Box 7
Tulsa, Ok. 74102

Veterans Administration Alcohol Service
810 Vermont Ave., NW
Washington, D.C. 10011

Wine Institute
717 Market St.
San Francisco, Ca. 94103

INDEX